A Note From Rick Renner

I am on a personal quest to see a "revival of the Bible" so people can establish their lives on a firm foundation that will stand strong and endure the test as end-time storm winds begin to intensify.

In order to experience a revival of the Bible in your personal life, it is important to take time each day to read, receive, and apply its truths to your life. James tells us that if we will continue in the perfect law of liberty — refusing to be forgetful hearers, but determined to be doers — we will be blessed in our ways. As you watch or listen to the programs in this series and work through this corresponding study guide, I trust you will search the Scriptures and allow the Holy Spirit to help you hear something new from God's Word that applies specifically to your life. I encourage you to be a doer of the Word He reveals to you. Whatever the cost, I assure you — it will be worth it.

> Thy words were found, and I did eat them;
> and thy word was unto me the joy and rejoicing of mine heart:
> for I am called by thy name, O Lord God of hosts.
> — Jeremiah 15:16

Your brother and friend in Jesus Christ,

Rick Renner

Unless otherwise indicated, all scripture quotations are taken from the *King James Version* of the Bible.

Scripture quotations marked (*NIV*) are taken from the *Holy Bible, New International Version®, NIV®* Copyright ©1973, 1978, 1984, 2011 by Biblica, Inc.® Used by permission. All rights reserved worldwide.

Scripture quotations marked (*NKJV*) are taken from the *New King James Version®*. Copyright © 1982 by Thomas Nelson. Used by permission. All rights reserved.

Scripture quotations marked (*NLT*) are taken from the Holy Bible, *New Living Translation*, copyright © 1996, 2004, 2015 by Tyndale House Foundation. Used by permission of Tyndale House Publishers, Inc., Carol Stream, Illinois 60188. All rights reserved.

Scriptures marked as (*GNT*) are taken from the **Good News Translation - Second Edition** © 1992 by American Bible Society. Used by permission.

Scripture quotations marked (*MSG*) are taken from *The Message*, copyright © 1993, 2002, 2018 by Eugene H. Peterson. Used by permission of NavPress. All rights reserved. Represented by Tyndale House Publishers, Inc.

Apostles and Prophets
Their Roles in the Past, Present, and the Last Days

Copyright © 2022 by Rick Renner
1814 W. Tacoma St.
Broken Arrow, OK 74012-1406

Published by Rick Renner Ministries
www.renner.org

ISBN 13: 978-1-6675-0304-2

eBook ISBN 13: 978-1-6675-0305-9

All rights reserved. No portion of this book may be reproduced or transmitted in any form or by any means — electronic, mechanical, photocopy, recording, scanning, or other — except for brief quotations in critical reviews or articles, without the prior written permission of the Publisher.

How To Use This Study Guide

This fifteen-lesson study guide corresponds to *"Apostles and Prophets" With Rick Renner* (Renner TV). Each lesson in this study guide covers a topic that is addressed during the program series, with questions and references supplied to draw you deeper into your own private study of the Scriptures on this subject.

To derive the most benefit from this study guide, consider the following:

First, watch or listen to the program prior to working through the corresponding lesson in this guide. (Programs can also be viewed at **renner.org** by clicking on the Media/Archives links or on our Renner Ministries YouTube channel.)

Second, take the time to look up the scriptures included in each lesson. Prayerfully consider their application to your own life.

Third, use a journal or notebook to make note of your answers to each lesson's Study Questions and Practical Application challenges.

Fourth, invest specific time in prayer and in the Word of God to consult with the Holy Spirit. Write down the scriptures or insights He reveals to you.

Finally, take action! Whatever the Lord tells you to do according to His Word, do it.

For added insights on this subject, it is recommended that you obtain Rick Renner's book *Apostles and Prophets: Their Roles in the Past, the Present, and the Last Days Church*. You may also select from Rick's other available resources by placing your order at **renner.org** or by calling 1-800-742-5593.

LESSON 1

TOPIC
Bad Theology and a Misuse of Terminology Makes a Mess for Everyone

SYNOPSIS
The fifteen lessons in this study titled *Apostles and Prophets* will focus on the following topics:

- Bad Theology and a Misuse of Terminology Makes a Mess for Everyone
- What an Apostle Is Not
- An Apostle Is Like an Admiral
- An Apostle Is Like a Special Package and a Travel Document
- An Apostle Is Like a Messenger, Envoy, or Ambassador
- How Many People Does the New Testament Identify as Apostles?
- What Are the Authenticating Signs of a Genuine Apostle? Part 1
- What Are the Authenticating Signs of a Genuine Apostle? Part 2
- Why Would Anyone Claim To Be an Apostle if He Wasn't an Apostle?
- What Is a Prophet?
- Four Pictures of Prophets
- How Prophets Do Not and Do Operate
- What and Who Are Intertestamental Prophets?
- How Many New Testament Prophets Are Actually Referred to in the New Testament?

- **What About False Prophets?**

What do you know about an apostle? How about a prophet? Do you believe there are still believers who function in these roles today? Like Rick, maybe you grew up in a denomination that taught that all apostles and prophets ceased to exist at the end of the Apostolic Age, and there is no such thing as an apostle or prophet in our day. For example, he thought for years that the term *apostle* applied only to a group of 12 legendary men who walked with Jesus some 2,000 years ago, and once that exclusive group died, it was the end of apostles.

For many, the theology they've heard growing up wouldn't sanction someone in the contemporary world being called an apostle. In fact, to call someone an apostle might seem like a blasphemous insult to the original Twelve. To people with this understanding, it is almost as if calling someone an apostle is tantamount to stealing a precious title that belongs exclusively to those first 12 apostles of Jesus.

Yet, regardless of what we believe, Christ has given the Church the gift of apostles and prophets, and their roles are still active in our time and our generation — and, thank God, they will be with us all the way to the end of the Church Age.

The emphasis of this lesson:

Although bad theology and a misuse of terminology has created much confusion for Christians regarding the offices of apostle and prophet, they are still viable roles filled by believers in the Church today. A person's hard work and innovative efforts alone do not automatically make them an apostle. Only God has the power and authority to appoint one to be an apostle.

How Did the Misunderstanding Start?

Back in the 1500s, scholarly Christians who spoke and read Latin began to use the word "missionary" for various reasons as a replacement for the word apostle. By definition, a missionary is *one who is sent by the Church to labor for the propagation of the faith in a place where it has not existed before or one who assists with the establishing of a gospel work*. Many missionaries are mightily anointed and called by God to help spread the Gospel and advance the Kingdom. They are truly a wonderful group of people who do honorable work for which we should all be grateful, but there is an important distinction that needs to be made.

The word *missionary* is not synonymous with the word *apostle*. These are two separate roles that are not the same thing. Although a small percentage of those whom we call missionaries are also apostles, it is imperative to understand that simply being a missionary does not always equate to being an apostle.

Unfortunately, as wonderful as many Christian denominations are, some have taught incorrect theology on this issue. For example, the church that Rick grew up in taught him how to serve and placed a vibrant love for God's Word in his heart. However, when it came to the supernatural gifts of the Spirit and the role of apostles and prophets, they were cessationists, meaning those in his church believed these supernatural gifts and roles ceased at the end of the Apostolic Age.

Strangely, these same Christians were very selective about exactly what things they believed ceased. Although they thought that the role of apostles and prophets had ended with the death of the original 12 apostles, they did still believe in the present-day role of evangelists, teachers, and pastors. And this is still a common belief held by some believers.

Thankfully, since the great outpouring of the Holy Spirit in the early 1900s, God has brought much correction to the Church in this area. More and more believers have come to understand that the gifts of the Spirit and *all* the fivefold ministry gifts Christ gave to the Church are still in full operation today. New Testament manifestations such as miracles, healings, signs and wonders, and the office of both prophets and apostles are being embraced and experienced more fully by the Body of Christ every day.

We've Gone From One Extreme to Another

There has definitely been an increased awareness of the gifts of the Spirit and the acceptance of prophets and apostles among believers today, but we seem to have swung to the other extreme. That is, it appears that an increasing number of Christians are being called an apostle or a prophet who are not.

For example, some individuals refer to themselves or others as "the apostle of prayer" or "the apostle of finances." Other people call themselves "the apostle of faith" or maybe "the apostle of marriage and parenting." Still others claim to be "the apostle of praise and worship." These, however, are all misuses of a very important term in the New Testament.

The fact is, many of these individuals are innovative pioneers in their area of ministry, and while they are certainly worthy of honor, respect, and esteem for their efforts, their accomplishments do not automatically make them an apostle. Being an ingenious groundbreaker and having a heart for spreading the Gospel does not mean you're an apostle.

When a term like *apostle* or *prophet* is repeatedly misused, people become confused and the word's true meaning becomes watered down and obscured. In some cases today, the use of the words "apostle" and "prophet" have become a badge of honor given to endorse a minister's hard work and pioneering efforts. Nevertheless, just because someone is hardworking, anointed, and great at what they do doesn't mean they are an apostle or prophet.

This Is Not a New Problem

Now, it should be noted that what we're talking about is nothing new. The apostle Paul was dealing with the same issue 2,000 years ago at the inception of the Church. Like today, there were many people claiming to be apostles who were not, and it was causing much confusion in the Early Church.

These pretentious individuals knew that if they could effectively convey the idea that they were apostles, it would give them a certain degree of leverage or weight in the Church that would result in personal gain or having an advantage over others. Thus, the apostle Paul took a strong stand against false apostles, exposing their exploitive actions and insincere motives and bringing correction to all who were involved.

The fact that Paul was addressing confusion regarding who was and wasn't an apostle back in the Church's infancy tells us this problem has been around for a long time. Paul would likely be astonished to see this confusion is still lingering in the Church today, nearly 2,000 years later. The number of individuals calling themselves apostles or who are being erroneously called apostles by others is unbelievable. The only difference between then and now is that people in Paul's day understood the meaning of the word "apostle" — a meaning that is vital for the Church to grasp today.

Ignorance Is Not Bliss — It's Dangerous

Make no mistake — the fivefold ministry gifts Christ gave the Church are very real and powerful, and they're still operating in the Church today. At the same time, we must also note that only a small percentage of the many people who claim to be apostles are actually apostles. To a great degree, the misuse of this term is primarily due to a lack of correct teaching on the subject. People simply do not understand what the word *apostle* really means.

It seems that even many pastors who are established in the Word have had difficulty deciphering the meaning of the word *apostle*. Out of ignorance, they have taught that an apostle is simply an energetic, innovative Christian leader who starts churches. And although the last part of that description comes a bit closer to the truth, it is still an oversimplified statement.

In the First Century, when the New Testament was being written and the Church was being established, the word *apostle* was an established and very well-known and understood term. In fact, it carried great authority even in the ambassadorial, educational, governmental, philosophical, and political world as well as in other secular spaces like the military. Many powerful concepts of the word *apostle* were instantly and automatically understood by people upon hearing it.

Therefore, how we use this term is very important. When a word like "apostle" that applies to a select few people is used too loosely, it gives the impression that apostles abound in the Body of Christ, and that is simply not the case.

The clear purpose of this series is to help us gain a biblical understanding of the gift of apostleship and the gift of a prophet. Moving forward, we will explore what an apostle was in the past, what apostles are in the present, and how apostles will function in the end-time Church.

STUDY QUESTIONS

> Study to shew thyself approved unto God, a workman that
> needeth not to be ashamed, rightly dividing the word of truth.
> — 2 Timothy 2:15

1. If you were given a test today and asked to describe an *apostle*, what would you say? If you grew up going to church, what kind of things did they teach about apostles and prophets?
2. Take a moment to read Hosea 4:6 and Ephesians 4:17 and 18. How do you think these verses apply to the importance of understanding what apostles and prophets really are?

PRACTICAL APPLICATION

> But be ye doers of the word, and not hearers only, deceiving your own selves.
> —James 1:22

1. Are you operating on what someone else told you about apostles (and prophets)? Or do you really know biblically and historically what they are?
2. It seems that several people have begun calling themselves things like "the apostle of prayer," "the apostle of finances," "the apostle of faith," or "the apostle of praise and worship." Have you ever heard individuals self-appoint themselves to positions like these? Does this strike you as normal or strange?
3. The fact is, only a small percentage of the many people who claim to be apostles are actually apostles. How do you think the misuse of this term and a lack of correct teaching on the subject has affected people's perspectives? How has it personally affected your view?

LESSON 2

TOPIC

What an Apostle Is Not

GREEK WORDS

1. "false apostles" — ψευδαπόστολος (*pseudapostolos*): a compound of ψευδής (*pseudes*) and ἀπόστολος (*apostolos*); the word ψευδής (*pseudes*) carries the idea of any type of falsehood, and it can picture a person who either intentionally or unintentionally projects a false

image of himself, someone who walks under some pretense, or one who projects an image that is untrue; a more up-to-date translation of the words "false apostles" could be pretend apostles or bogus apostles

SYNOPSIS

As we noted in our first lesson, there are many individuals today who are erroneously calling themselves apostles and prophets. Although most people are likely sincere in thinking they are using these titles correctly, they are mistaken. They simply don't understand the true meaning of these words because they lack solid, biblical teaching on the subject or have received bad theology.

The truth is, if Christians today were asked to provide a description of what an apostle is, most would say that an apostle is a Christian leader who's innovative and pioneering. Occasionally, someone might add that an apostle is someone who starts churches, and while that is closer to the truth, it's still an oversimplification of what an apostle is.

Think about it. How many people do you know who have started a church? Does starting a church mean that person is an apostle? If it does, then that would mean there are numerous apostles in the Body of Christ today, but that's not the case. Therefore, there must be more to the meaning of the word "apostle" than just someone who starts churches. That is exactly what we are going to discover in this lesson.

The emphasis of this lesson:

Having a strong heart desire to see the Gospel advance and churches established is wonderful, but just because a person has an apostolic heart doesn't mean he is called by Christ to be a fivefold ministry apostle. It may be that God is using those desires to direct that person to where he should be serving in the Church or in someone else's ministry.

When it Comes to the Fivefold Ministry Gifts, Many of God's People Are Confused

For centuries, the subject of apostleship wasn't deemed important or necessary to understand, and no one offered any sound teaching on the topic. As a result, generations of people don't know what the word "apostle" means or what an apostle does. Rick shared a situation he experienced that clearly demonstrates just how much confusion there is regarding the fivefold ministry gifts Paul talks about in Ephesians 4:11-13.

Several years ago, Rick was at a conference for average church attenders where he was scheduled to speak (note: this was not a ministry conference for those in fivefold ministry positions). Just before he was to begin, the speaker who preceded him asked the crowd, "How many of you here today are called into fivefold ministry?"

Suddenly, hands flew into the air all around the auditorium. As Rick looked to see how many were raised, to his amazement it looked like 80 to 90 percent of the crowd had lifted their hands. In other words, out of the hundreds and hundreds of people present, virtually everyone in the building said they were called to be either an apostle, prophet, evangelist, pastor, or teacher. Keep in mind, this was not a pastoral or ministry leader's meeting; it was just a regular church conference.

The fact of the matter is, 80 to 90 percent of those conference attendees were not called into fivefold ministry. The gifts of apostle, prophet, evangelist, pastor, and teacher are much rarer than those believers — and most believers — realize.

The overuse of fivefold ministry names has given many people the incorrect impression that these rare gifts can be found in large numbers in the Church. Consequently, it has led people to believe they can call themselves by any title they wish, and sadly, this has also resulted in an overall diminished awe, respect, and weightiness for the fivefold ministry gifts.

What Does a Strong Heart Desire Actually Tell Us?

If we look around the Church today, many have an *apostolic heart*. In other words, they have a strong desire to see the Gospel advance and churches established, which is a wonderful, God-given passion. But just because a person has an apostolic heart, it doesn't mean they are an apostle and have been called by Christ to the fivefold ministry position of an apostle.

Some people have been given an apostolic heart by God because He has called them to serve alongside a true apostle. Think about it — every apostle needs people who have apostolic hearts to help him. So, having an apostolic heart alone doesn't mean you're an apostle.

If you have a strong desire to help the Church be established in other places, it could be God's way of providing you direction. More than likely, He's showing you where you should be serving in the Church or in someone else's ministry.

How about the office of the *prophet*? Many have a prophetic tendency, but that does not make them a prophet. Having the Christ-given, fivefold ministry gift of a prophet and having a prophetic leaning are not the same thing. As Paul said in First Corinthians 12, some of us are given the gift of prophecy by the Holy Spirit, but he didn't say that prophesying made us a fivefold ministry prophet.

If you have a strong leaning or tendency toward prophecy, it could be God's way of providing you direction as to where you should serve in the Church or in someone else's ministry. Additionally, He may be cultivating the fivefold gift of the prophet in you, and if He is, He will reveal it in time. In the meantime, know that having a prophetic tendency does not automatically make you a prophet.

What about being an *evangelist*? It is clear from Jesus' Great Commission that we should all have a heart for the lost (*see* Matthew 28:18-20). It is God's greatest desire that all people come to the full knowledge of the truth and be saved (*see* 1 Timothy 2:1-4), and He wants us to be a part of seeing that happen. However, having a heart for the lost and being called by God to the office of an evangelist are not necessarily the same.

If you have a strong desire to reach the lost, perhaps the anointing of the evangelist is developing in you. Or it could simply be God's way of providing you direction as to where you should serve in the Church or in someone else's ministry. Again, having a heart for the lost and being an actual fivefold ministry evangelist are not the same.

There is also the gift of the *pastor*. Many believers have a heart to help care for others, but that doesn't necessarily make them a Christ-given, fivefold ministry pastor. We should all have caring hearts and help bear one another's burdens (*see* Galatians 6:2), but simply having a caring heart does not mean a person is called to be a fivefold ministry pastor.

Yes, it's possible that the anointing of a pastor is developing in you, and if that's the case, the Holy Spirit will confirm it in time. In the meantime, if your desire to care for others is strong, it may simply be God's way of showing you where you should serve in the Church or in someone else's ministry.

Also consider the fivefold gift of a *teacher*. Clearly, many have a heart for teaching the Bible. They love God's Word and love the opportunity to share the scriptural insights they've learned with others. But loving to teach the Bible and being called to function in the role of a Christ-given, fivefold teacher are not necessarily the same.

If you have a strong heart desire to teach God's Word, it could be that God is using it to direct you to where you should be serving in the Church or in someone else's ministry. If He is developing the fivefold ministry gift of a teacher in you, He will make it clear in time.

The bottom line: Don't let the leaning in your heart cause you to automatically assume you are called to an area of fivefold ministry. Seek the presence of God and ask Him to show you what He's doing in your heart. He said, "I will instruct you and teach you in the way you should go; I will counsel you with my loving eye on you" (Psalm 32:8, *NIV*). If God is calling you to one of the fivefold areas of ministry, He will make it clear to you.

Paul Addressed the Issue of 'False Apostles'

As we saw in our first lesson, there were people in the Early Church who claimed to be apostles who were not. The apostle Paul got wind of what was going on and took the opportunity to address the issue of false prophets in his second letter to the believers at Corinth.

In Greek, the phrase "false apostles" is a translation of the word *pseudapostolos*, which is a compound of the words *pseudes* and *apostolos*. The word *pseudes* carries the idea of *any type of falsehood*, and it can picture *a person who either intentionally or unintentionally projects a false image of himself*. This is someone who walks under some pretense or one who projects an image that is untrue. The word *apostolos* is the term for *apostle*. When these two words are compounded to form the word *pseudapostolos*, it describes "*false apostles.*" A more up-to-date translation of this term could be *pretend apostles* or *bogus apostles*.

There were so many people in the First Century who were *pretend apostles* or *bogus apostles* that the Early Church created a criterion they could use to determine who was a real apostle and who was not. The same criteria they used then is the criteria we need to use today.

In the next lesson, we're going to begin looking into history to see the multiple meanings of the word "apostle."

STUDY QUESTIONS

> Study to shew thyself approved unto God, a workman that needeth not to be ashamed, rightly dividing the word of truth.
> — 2 Timothy 2:15

1. Carefully read Paul's words in Ephesians 4:11-13 and name the five specific gifts Jesus gave to the Church after He was resurrected back to life. For what reasons did the Lord give these gifts to the Body of Christ?
2. According to First Corinthians 12:7-11, what are the 9 gifts of the Spirit? What does Paul compare these different gifts to in First Corinthians 12:12, 13, and 27? What do his words of caution in First Corinthians 12:14-26 say to you personally?

PRACTICAL APPLICATION

> But be ye doers of the word, and not hearers only, deceiving your own selves.
> — James 1:22

1. After reading through the section about having a strong heart desire, what kind of leaning(s) do *you* have? Do you desire to see churches planted or passionately teach God's Word? Do you have a tendency toward the prophetic or a strong desire to see people saved? Of the five gifts, where would you say your heart desires tend to lean?
2. Be careful not to let the leaning in your heart cause you to automatically assume you are called to an area of fivefold ministry. Take time now to seek the presence of God and ask Him to show you what He's doing in your heart (*see* Psalm 139:23,24; Jeremiah 17:9,10). He said, "I will instruct you and teach you in the way you should go; I will counsel you with my loving eye on you" (Psalm 32:8 *NIV*). If God is calling you to one of the fivefold areas of ministry, ask Him to make it clear to you.

LESSON 3

TOPIC
An Apostle Is Like an Admiral

SCRIPTURES
1. **2 Corinthians 10:16** — To preach the gospel in the regions beyond you, and not to boast in another man's line of things made ready to our hand.
2. **Acts 13:13** — Now when Paul and his company loosed from Paphos, they came to Perga in Pamphylia: and John departing from them returned to Jerusalem.

GREEK WORDS
1. "apostle" — ἀπόστολος (*apostolos*): a compound of ἀπό (*apo*) and στέλλω (*stello*); the preposition ἀπό (*apo*) means away and στέλλω (*stello*) means to send; compounded, it forms the word ἀπόστολος (*apostolos*), and it pictures one who is sent away

SYNOPSIS
In Lesson 1, we saw what happens when we receive bad theology and don't have an accurate understanding of what an apostle and a prophet is. As a result of the confusion over these terms, they have been misused and abused and have been greatly diminished in power.

Then in Lesson 2, we took a closer look at who is *not* an apostle. In fact, we learned that just because a person has a heart for specific aspects of being an apostle, a prophet, an evangelist, a pastor, or a teacher, it doesn't mean they're called by God to fill one of those fivefold ministry positions. Many times, God gives us certain desires to direct us where and with whom we are to serve in the Church.

In this lesson, we're going to begin to excavate the meaning of the word "apostle." Although you may have an idea of its definition, you will likely be surprised by the historical significance of this term — both *before* and *during* the time of the New Testament. Are you ready? Let's dive deep into the ancient roots of this amazing word — the word "apostle."

The emphasis of this lesson:

One early use of the word *apostolos* (apostle) denoted an admiral, the fleet of ships that traveled with him, and the specialized crew and cargo that accompanied him as he went to colonize uncivilized territories. In the New Testament, an apostle was someone who was selected, empowered, and invested with authority by the Church or by the Lord Himself and then dispatched to accomplish a special task.

The Basic Meaning of the Word 'Apostle'

When we journey back in time, we find the earliest usages and meaning of the word "apostle." It is the Greek word *apostolos*, a compound of *apo* and *stello*. The preposition *apo* means *away*, and the word *stello* means *to send*. When compounded, these words become *apostolos*, the word for "apostle," which is used frequently throughout the New Testament, and it pictures *one who is sent away*.

Interestingly, while the word *apostolos* is used 80 times in the New Testament, the root of *apostolos* — the word *apostello* — is used 132 times in the New Testament and more than 700 times in the Septuagint, which is the Greek translation of the Old Testament. The reason this is important is because when a word is used that frequently, it is very easy to establish its meaning.

How Did Ancient Greek Writers Use the Word Apostle?

Legendary writers from antiquity helped set the stage for how the word "apostle" would be used in the New Testament. For instance, the Greek playwright **Euripides** and historian **Thucydides** used *apostolos* (apostle) to describe *important packages that were sent*. These special packages were sent by powerful people and contained very important contents.

The Greek philosopher **Aristotle** used the word *apostolos* to picture *the seeing off or sending away of important individuals*, and Greek historian **Herodotus** used it to describe *a high-powered ambassador who had been sent to represent a government or king*.

Moreover, the Greek historian, philosopher, magistrate, and ambassador **Plutarch** used the word *apostolos* to depict *the sending away of a trade ship filled with cargo*. Similarly, Greek philosopher **Plato** and historian

Polybius used *apostolos* to depict *a huge ship that was fully loaded with cargo and a specialized crew that accompanied an admiral who was venturing into new territory to construct a new community.*

Furthermore, the philosopher and speechwriter **Lucian**, along with the historian **Lysias, Demosthenes,** and **Plutarch**, used the word *apostolos* to depict *a fully equipped, large fleet that was sent on an expedition to a new territory.* These are all various ways in which the word "apostle" — the Greek word *apostolos* — was used before the time of the New Testament.

Using these meanings as a foundation, the word "apostle" in the New Testament depicts *individuals who were appointed, empowered, and invested with authority by either the leadership of the Church or by the Lord Himself.* They were dispatched to represent the leadership of the Church or Christ and carry out a special work of establishing the Church in places where it had not previously existed.

Thus, the word "apostle" (*apostolos*) categorically had no other application in New Testament times except this one. An apostle never referred to one who was self-appointed, but rather to one who was selected, empowered, and invested with authority by Church leaders or by the Lord Himself and then dispatched to accomplish a special task.

The Word 'Apostle' Was Synonymous With Sea Travel

Now it is important to point out that long before the word *apostolos* was ever used in the New Testament to describe an apostle, it was a very specific maritime term connected to seafaring.

Circling back to the Greek philosopher Plato and the historian Polybius, we see they used *apostolos* to depict *a huge ship that was fully loaded with cargo and a specialized crew that accompanied an admiral who was venturing into new territory to construct a new community.* Thus, **the admiral of a fleet of ships** was called an "apostle" (*apostolos*).

Again, keeping with this maritime theme, Plutarch used the word *apostolos* to depict *the sending away of a trade ship filled with cargo.* Thus, the word *apostolos* also described **the fleet of ships** that traveled with the admiral.

In addition to being known as the admiral of a fleet of ships and the ships themselves, the word *apostolos* also described **the specialized crew who**

accompanied and assisted the admiral as he sailed to locate territories where civilization was nonexistent and then construct a replica of their own life, language, and culture there. And the word "apostle" (*apostolos*) also described **the supplies and cargo needed to sustain the crew and to establish civilization where it had been nonexistent.**

So, the ancient word *apostolos*, which is where we get the word "apostle," was used in a maritime sense to picture a highly powered admiral and his specialized crew, who were sent off with all the cargo and belongings needed to sustain them in order to establish a civilization where it had been non-existent.

An Apostle Always Traveled With a Trained Crew

That admiral — or *apostle* — along with his specialized crew set sail to virgin lands where they would disembark and settle down to establish life as they believed it should be. As soon as they went ashore, the admiral (or *apostle*) became the onsite leader who led the entire crew as they established and constructed a new community that had never existed before. Thus, the admiral and his apostolic crew were *colonists*.

Dispatched under the leadership of their admiral, these specially trained colonists were sent to spread their culture and influence across the world. Because of the bravery needed to colonize a new region, colonists like these were considered heroes.

To fulfill their task of colonizing a new territory, the admiral needed in his fleet associates, assistants, secretaries, and all the resources necessary to carry out their assignment. So, when the admiral disembarked from his fleet of ships and walked down the plank into a new region, he didn't walk by himself. He was accompanied by his team members or apostolic crew.

Due to the very nature of the admiral's assignment, it was impossible for him to travel alone or to attempt to do the job by himself. Therefore, he always had an apostolic crew that traveled with him. To successfully oversee the construction of a brand-new colony or civilization where it had never existed before, the admiral (apostle) had to think as a team leader and depend on his fellow team members to come together and each do their part.

Colonizing New Territories Was Their Goal

Once on land, the admiral (or *apostolos*), along with his apostolic team immediately surveyed the new location to identify challenges as well as determine all the advantages they could find. After this initial assessment was complete, the apostolic crew began the difficult process of transforming a strange and uncivilized land. This required an unwavering commitment to the task, endurance to withstand opposition, and stamina to brave the obstacles.

Their purpose and goal was to replicate life as they believed it should be — a process we would call *total colonization*. Exactly how long the admiral and his team remained in one location depended on the challenges that arose in each place they ventured. Some regions were easier to colonize than others. Whatever the case, the admiral didn't move to the next location with his team until the process of colonization was well underway.

Once the new region was settled and the process of colonization was substantially far along, the admiral, along with his specialized crew, reboarded the ship to set sail for another location to repeat the process again.

Are you beginning to see how all this fits together with the ministry of a New Testament apostle? If we were to stop right here and go no further, we could likely say that most people have already grasped a better understanding of how the meaning of the Greek word *apostolos* — the word "apostle" — was understood by believers in the Early Church. When they heard the word *apostolos*, they knew it referred to a high-powered individual dispatched either by the Lord or by the Church to launch out with a team into virgin territory where the Gospel had never been preached in order to establish the Church where it had never existed before.

The Apostle Paul Had Many Helpers

When Paul wrote his second letter to the believers in Corinth, he told them that he and his team were going "to preach the gospel in the regions beyond you…" (2 Corinthians 10:16). He was launching out into untouched places where no one had ever worked before, which is exactly what apostles are called to do.

It is important to note that when Paul went on his apostolic journeys, he never went alone. Acts 13:13 tells us that Paul travelled with his "company," and when we read the entire book of Acts, we see that his travel companions included Barnabas, Silas, John Mark, Timothy, Erastus, Sopater, Aristarchus, Secundus, Gaius, Tychicus, Trophimus, Luke, and Aquila and Priscilla.

Although Paul was a mightily anointed, legendary apostle (*apostolos*), he could not accomplish the work alone. Just as any other successful admiral in pre-New Testament times, he needed the side-by-side participation of others who were a part of his apostolic crew.

When Paul and his team arrived, they disembarked into the region to preach the Gospel, drive back darkness, and press forward to spiritually colonize a once dark region. Their united efforts continued until they replicated the life, language, and culture of the Church in this place where it had never been established before. The length of time that Paul and his crew spent in each location varied, depending on the difficulty of the tasks. Some places required a short period of time, while others required longer stays with much more intensive labor.

In our next lesson, we're going to explore yet another meaning of the word "apostle" and see how legendary Greek writers used it to describe *a package, a travel document,* or a *passport.*

STUDY QUESTIONS

Study to shew thyself approved unto God, a workman that needeth not to be ashamed, rightly dividing the word of truth.
— 2 Timothy 2:15

1. Using the historical facts and insights presented in this lesson, write down the meaning of the word "apostle" in your own words.
2. What are some of the ways ancient Greek writers used the word *apostolos* (apostle) before the time of the New Testament? Which usage is most intriguing to you? Why?
3. According to Matthew 10:1-16, what were Jesus' basic instructions to the original 12 apostles when He sent them out?

PRACTICAL APPLICATION

> But be ye doers of the word, and not hearers only,
> deceiving your own selves.
> — James 1:22

1. Taking together all that you learned in this lesson about the meaning of the word "apostle" (*apostolos*), how does it help you better understand and appreciate what the apostle Paul and other New Testament apostles actually did — and still do?

2. Now that you know a little bit more about the work of an apostle, how do you think you would do at fulfilling this fivefold ministry role? What would you most enjoy doing as an apostle and why?

LESSON 4

TOPIC

An Apostle Is Like a Special Package and a Travel Document

SCRIPTURES

1. **Romans 15:29** — And I am sure that, when I come unto you, I shall come in the fulness of the blessing of the gospel of Christ.
2. **1 Corinthians 16:9** — For a great door and effectual is opened unto me, and there are many adversaries.

GREEK WORDS

1. "great" — μεγάλη (*megale*): something enormous or massive
2. "door" — θύρα (*thura*): a door that was usually locked shut with a heavy bolt that slid through rings attached to the door and the frame; this kind of door was normally sealed tight, but Paul said that what had been sealed tight for others swung wide open for him
3. "effectual" — ἐνεργής (*energes*): extremely powerful and filled with possibilities

4. "patience" — ὑπομονή (*hupomene*): to stay or abide; to remain in one's spot; to keep a position; to resolve to maintain territory gained; in a military sense, it pictures soldiers ordered to maintain their positions even in the face of opposition; to defiantly stick it out regardless of pressures mounted against it; staying power; hang-in-there power; the attitude that holds out, holds on, outlasts, perseveres, and hangs in there, never giving up, refusing to surrender to obstacles, and turning down every opportunity to quit; it pictures one who is under a heavy load but refuses to bend, break, or surrender because he is convinced that the territory, promise, or principle under assault rightfully belongs to him

SYNOPSIS

In our previous lesson, we learned that an apostle is like an admiral, his fleet of ships that travel with him, and his specialized apostolic crew and cargo that accompanies him. Once the apostle and his crew board the ships, they set sail for virgin territory where they work together to establish the Church.

The goal of any apostle and his team is to replicate the life, the language, and the culture of the Church in an area where it is nonexistent. Once the Church is well on its way to being established, the apostle and key members of his crew get back on board their ships and set sail for more new territory where they can repeat the process again.

This lesson will take a closer look at how an apostle is like a special package that is sent or like a travel document, permitting him and his team to travel where others cannot gain access.

The emphasis of this lesson:

An apostle is like a special package containing important contents. He is also like a travel document or passport who has the anointing of God on his life, enabling him to go where others can't go. Doors that are normally closed for others miraculously open for an apostle. Once he enters these uncharted territories, he is anointed with endurance to stand against all assaults that oppose him and his team and to stay put until the job is done.

An Apostle Is Like a 'Divine Package'

What else does history tell us about the unique meaning of the word *apostolos* (apostle)? The Greek playwright Euripides and the historian Thucydides used *apostolos* to describe *important packages that were sent or special packages sent by powerful people that contained powerful and important contents*. Thus, we can infer that an apostle in the Early Church and today is a *divine package sent by Christ or the Church that carries the anointing of God*. A real apostle is filled with God's anointing to do whatever is necessary when he shows up to the place he has been sent.

This explains why the apostle Paul could confidently tell the believers in Rome, "And I am sure that, when I come unto you, I shall come in the fulness of the blessing of the gospel of Christ" (Romans 15:29). Paul knew that as an apostle he was sent by Jesus Christ as a special, divine package filled with power and the anointing of God to accomplish everything he needed to, wherever he was sent. The same is true of all apostles.

An Apostle Is Like a 'Travel Document or Passport'

Interestingly, the word *apostolos* — the Greek word for "apostle" — was so closely linked to travel that it eventually became synonymous with the concept of *a travel document* or *a passport* that one would use to move from one country to another. Today, if a person wants to exit a nation and travel internationally, he or she must present a passport or a travel document, which is the equivalent of a passport, to cross that boarder and enter a new territory. These requirements were very similar in the ancient world.

In antiquity, world travel was very difficult, very dangerous, and extremely expensive. Widespread travel was primarily done in the interest of warfare and diplomacy, for visiting religious sites, or to receive medical care for a family member or for oneself. That said, it would have been very difficult — or nearly impossible — to travel without having a passport or a travel document. The Greeks called these papers an *apostolos*. But even with an *apostolos*, a person's freedom to move about was still restricted at times. Nevertheless, it did guarantee certain rights that other travelers didn't have.

Just as a travel document or a passport is a door-opener that is needed to journey into new regions or territories, this additional ancient use of the word *apostolos* informs us that an apostle is anointed like a travel document or a passport, and doors open for him and his ministry that may not ordinarily open for others.

Indeed, this apostolic anointing enables an individual to have supernatural authority to pass into new geographical regions and territories that would normally be difficult, if not impossible, for others to enter. This means a bona fide apostle is graced and supernaturally anointed to cross difficult barriers into new regions so he and his team can colonize a new territory for the Kingdom of God.

Their anointing takes them into hard-to-penetrate regions and keeps them there. Once they're in place, an apostle becomes like a divine bulldozer that clears demonic rubbish out of the way, enabling the process of establishing the Church where it has never been established before to begin.

The Apostolic Anointing Opens Doors That Are Normally Sealed Shut

During the ministry of the apostle Paul, he wrote to the Corinthian church and said, "For a great door and effectual is opened unto me, and there are many adversaries" (1 Corinthians 16:9). It seems that God was regularly opening doors of ministry opportunity for Paul that were closed to others.

In this verse, the word "great" is the Greek word *megale*, which describes *something enormous or massive*. And the Greek word for "door" is *thura*, which was used to describe *a door that was usually locked shut with a heavy bolt that slid through rings attached to the door and the frame*. This kind of door was normally sealed tight, but Paul said that what had been sealed tight for others swung wide open for him. Furthermore, he described this door as "effectual," which is a translation of the Greek word *energes*, meaning it was *extremely powerful and filled with possibilities*.

Taking into account the original Greek meaning of this verse, it is the equivalent of Paul saying, "An enormous, massive door that is usually sealed shut for others has suddenly swung open for me with divine and great possibilities." The apostolic anointing on his life was like a supernatural passport enabling him to enter new territories.

Paul then informed the church that within this massive door of opportunity, "…There are many adversaries" (1 Corinthians 16:9). This is valuable to know, because very often when there is an amazing opportunity to do something for God, we can run into "adversaries" on the other side of that achievement. These adversaries may consist of difficult challenges, unexpected opposition, and enemy interference.

'Patience' Is One of the Primary Signs of a Genuine Apostle

It is interesting to note that one of the first signs Paul cites as a confirmation of being an apostle is the ability to endure difficult places. For example, in Second Corinthians 12:12, he said, "Truly the signs of an apostle were wrought among you in all patience, in signs, and wonders, and mighty deeds."

Although most people immediately focus on signs, wonders, and mighty deeds, the first descriptive marking of an apostle Paul mentioned is "patience." This word is a translation of the Greek word *hupomene*, which is *the ability to stay or abide* or *to remain in one's spot*. It means *to keep a position* or *to resolve to maintain territory gained*. In a military sense, it pictures soldiers who are ordered to maintain their positions even in the face of opposition.

Indeed, those who are called to do apostolic work are often assigned to regions that are not for the faint of heart. The devil launches all kinds of attacks against them, which is why they need *patience* — the Greek word *hupomene*. This term carries the idea of *defiantly sticking it out regardless of pressures mounted against it*. It is *staying power, hang-in-there power*, and *the attitude that holds out, holds on, outlasts, perseveres, and hangs in there, never giving up, refusing to surrender to obstacles, and turning down every opportunity to quit*. One operating in "patience" is one who is under a heavy load but refuses to bend, break, or surrender because he is convinced that the territory, promise, or principle under assault rightfully belongs to him.

Paul lists this kind of supernatural endurance as one of the chief signs of a genuine apostle. This means that a real apostle doesn't "tuck his tail and run" when times get tough. Once he has walked through an open door, he is anointed to stay there even if that open door comes with hostile adversaries.

A Quick Recap of This Lesson

So, when New Testament ears heard the word *apostolos* — the Greek word for "apostle" — they immediately knew it depicted a person who, like *a travel document or a passport*, was supernaturally anointed to journey into regions that were barred from others or that were otherwise hard to penetrate. This explains why it was possible for the early apostles to travel far across the world at a time when travel was extremely difficult and dangerous.

Clearly, apostles have a door-opening anointing that enables them to journey beyond where others have ventured and into regions where no man has labored. They possess a divine grace that supernaturally enables them to stay put despite the adversities or the hostile enemies they encounter so they can fulfill their calling to preach the Gospel and establish the Church where it has been previously nonexistent.

The fact that apostles thrive in difficult regions is one reason the Church in comfortable parts of the world seems to be less familiar with living apostles than they are with the other fivefold ministry gifts. Apostles primarily function and thrive on the front lines of spiritual battle where others are not anointed to go.

In our next lesson, we will look at how this word *apostolos* has also been used to depict a spiritual messenger with the divine ability to take others into new spiritual realms and dimensions.

STUDY QUESTIONS

> **Study to shew thyself approved unto God, a workman that needeth not to be ashamed, rightly dividing the word of truth.**
> **— 2 Timothy 2:15**

1. In this lesson, we learned that an apostle is like *a package filled with God's anointing to do whatever is necessary when he shows up*. Do you know anyone today that is functioning as an apostle in this way? If so, who is it and how have their efforts affected your life?
2. Apostles are not the only ones who need *patience* — all of us need the "mother of all virtues," including *you*. What do the following verses say about patience? Where does it come from? How is it developed, and why do you need it in your life?

- Galatians 5:22,23
- Colossians 1:11,12
- Hebrews 10:36
- James 1:2-4
- Romans 5:3-5

PRACTICAL APPLICATION

> But be ye doers of the word, and not hearers only, deceiving your own selves.
> —James 1:22

1. God has given apostles a door-opening anointing, enabling them to cross barriers into new places to advance the Gospel. What does the Bible say about God opening and closing doors? Read Revelation 3:7,8; Colossians 4:2,3; Malachi 3:8-11; Acts 5:18-20. What is the Holy Spirit showing you in these passages?
2. Where do you need God to open a door for you? Pray and ask Him to show you anything you need to do in order to see God open THE door He wants you to walk through.
3. Paul said that with a massive door of opportunity, "…there are many adversaries" (1 Corinthians 16:9). What adversaries — oppositions or hindrances — are you facing right now? Pray for God's wisdom and His supernatural involvement to remove every roadblock that is hindering you from doing what He's asking you to do.

LESSON 5

TOPIC
An Apostle Is Like a Messenger, Envoy, or Ambassador

SCRIPTURES
1. **Galatians 1:11,12** — But I certify you, brethren, that the gospel which was preached of me is not after man. For I neither received it of man, neither was I taught it, but by the revelation of Jesus Christ.

GREEK WORDS
1. "revelation" — ἀποκάλυψις (*apokalupsis*): a compound of the preposition ἀπο (*apo*) and κάλυψις (*kalupsis*); the preposition ἀπο (*apo*) means away and κάλυψις (*kalupsis*) depicts something that is covered, hidden, or veiled; when compounded to form the word ἀποκάλυψις (*apokalupsis*), it pictures an obstructive covering that has been suddenly and supernaturally removed, and what was on the other side of that obstruction is now uncovered, unhidden, and unveiled

SYNOPSIS
Thus far, we have learned that bad theology regarding the roles of apostles and prophets has led to the misuse, and in some cases the abuse, of these terms. This diminishes their God-given authority and the power of these offices.

We have also seen that the word "apostle" (*apostolos*) had multiple meanings in the ancient world. Historically, the title "apostle" was synonymous with that of *an admiral* who set sail with an apostolic crew into virgin territory to colonize a new region. The word "apostle" could also describe *important packages* that were sent by powerful people and contained powerful and important contents. Thus, an apostle in the Early Church and today is like *a divine package sent by Christ or the Church that carries the anointing of God.* He is filled with God's power to do whatever is needed when he shows up.

Moreover, the word "apostle" was also used to depict *a travel document* or *a passport* that enabled people to enter territories that were normally restricted to others. This is exactly what New Testament apostles like the apostle Paul were anointed to do. They were supernaturally given entrance into places others were denied access.

Next, we are going to look at how an apostle is a special messenger, empowered with the divine ability to take others into new spiritual realms and dimensions.

The emphasis of this lesson:

The word *apostolos* (apostle) also carries the meaning of a special messenger who has the ability to take others into new spiritual realms and dimensions. Thus, the anointing on a New Testament apostle's life enables him to take believers to greater depths of spiritual revelation and understanding than others will likely experience.

An Apostle Has the Ability to Take Believers Into Higher Realms of Revelation

Over time the word *apostolos* — our New Testament word for an apostle — took on another very important meaning. It became a common term for *a person who was especially gifted with special insight and revelation and who was sent by the gods as their special messenger to people.* The ancient Greek world stood in awe of such *apostolos* messengers and believed that gods had endued them with special wisdom and revelation that enabled them to take others with them into higher realms of revelation and understanding.

This perception was very familiar to the ears of those who heard the word *apostolos* in biblical times. Hence, New Testament believers understood that an apostle was one who possessed special insight and revelation, and if they would stay near to that apostle, he could lead them into new spiritual dimensions that they could not get to by themselves.

This extraordinary apostolic ability to access higher spiritual realms is alluded to by the apostle Paul in Galatians 1:11 and 12, where he wrote, "But I certify you, brethren, that the gospel which was preached of me is not after man. For I neither received it of man, neither was I taught it, but by the revelation of Jesus Christ." Clearly, Paul had been given insights into the things of God that no one else had received.

Paul Received 'Revelation' Directly From Jesus

Notice Paul said he was taught "by the revelation of Jesus Christ." The word "revelation" here is the Greek word *apokalupsis*, which is a compound of the preposition *apo* and the word *kalupsis*. The word *apo* means *away*, and *kalupsis* depicts *something that is covered, hidden, or veiled*. When compounded to form the word *apokalupsis*, it pictures *an obstructive covering that has been suddenly and supernaturally removed*, and what was on the other side of that obstruction is now uncovered, unhidden, and unveiled.

If we apply this meaning to what Paul wrote in Galatians 1:11 and 12, it tells us that God supernaturally enabled Paul to see what others had never seen before. That was part of his equipment as an apostle — to go spiritually where others had not gone. This agrees entirely with what Jesus told Paul (then called Saul) when He first appeared to him on the road to Damascus.

As Paul shared the story of His encounter with Jesus with King Agrippa, he noted that Jesus told him, "Now get to your feet! For I have appeared to you to appoint you as my servant and witness. Tell people that you have seen me, and tell them what I will show you in the future" (Acts 26:16 *NLT*).

Stop and think about how blessed the New Testament churches were at Rome, Corinth, Galatia, Ephesus, Colossae, Philippi, Thessalonica, and other locations because of the insights and revelations they received by being in relationship with Paul. By hanging on to his apostolic coattails and being in partnership with him, those churches heard amazing truths that other churches didn't have access to. They soared to spiritual heights others couldn't attain by themselves.

Apostles Provide Exponential Access to the Things of God

To be clear, all believers have access to the Father and to a certain level of the spirit realm and divine revelation. However, Christ's gift of the apostle unlocks the door to even greater levels of revelation. This is the principle Jesus Himself gives us in Matthew's gospel:

> **Whoever welcomes God's messenger because he is God's messenger, will share in his reward. And whoever welcomes a good man because he is good, will share in his reward.**
> — **Matthew 10:41 (*GNT*)**

When a church is near a genuine apostle (*apostolos*), it has the opportunity to journey with him into new spiritual realms and dimensions. If an individual or church grabs hold of an apostle's spiritual coattails and stays connected with him, the anointing on that apostle's life will take that person or church into new and higher realms of revelation.

That is what this word *apostolos* — the Greek word for "apostle" — tells us. Are you seeing how important it is that we understand the meaning of this word? It had such a significant bearing on the idea of apostleship in the New Testament.

Apostles Are God's Special Dignitaries

In addition to all that we have seen, there is yet another meaning of the word *apostolos*. Early records show it was also the very word used by ancient Greek writers to describe powerful dignitaries, such as *an envoy* or *an ambassador*, who were chosen to represent a government or a king. In the Church's case, an apostle is anointed to be *God's envoy* or *God's ambassador*.

The Greek philosopher Aristotle used the word *apostolos* to picture *the seeing off or sending away of important individuals*. Greek historian Herodotus used this term to describe *a high-powered ambassador* who had been sent to represent a government or king.

Thus, the word *apostolos* was used to picture an envoy who was sent to do business on behalf of the one who sent him. Likewise, it also depicted a personal representative, an emissary, a messenger, an agent, a diplomat, or an ambassador. This means that apostles in the Church were — and are — individuals who are dispatched by God as His chosen representatives, and they hold an elevated rank in the Church. All this additional meaning is packed into the word *apostolos*, which is translated as "apostle" in the New Testament.

Understanding the Role of Ambassadors in the Ancient World

Now, it is important for you to understand the vital role these dignitaries played in the ancient world. During that time, the word *apostolos* was used to refer to an ambassador or a high-ranking diplomat dispatched to represent the government or king who sent him on a specific mission in a foreign city or land. As the government's or king's representative, these *apostolos* held the highest diplomatic rank that could be given.

You may be wondering, *what is the relevance for this fact regarding the ministry of New Testament apostles?* That is a good question. The fact that *apostolos* held such a high rank means Christ-given apostles also hold an especially high rank in the Body of Christ, and in God's view, they are individuals who are dispatched by Him as His chosen representatives. Isn't it amazing how these historical insights have such relevance to the ministry of an apostle?

The fact is, the word *apostolos* — translated as "apostle" in the New Testament — had a lengthy history and carried a wide range of important meanings, all of which overlapped and interrelated with each other. Let's take a moment and sum up the four specific meanings of the word *apostolos* that we've covered so far.

Four Meanings of the Word 'Apostle' (*Apostolos*)

Number One: An apostle was like an *admiral* who traveled with a specialized fleet of ships and a specialized crew who accompanied and assisted him as he sailed into open seas to locate territories where civilization was nonexistent.

Once the admiral made it to uncharted land, he and his crew disembarked and began to replicate life, language, and culture as they believed it should be. This included building an infrastructure of roads, buildings, houses, and temples in the new territory.

Here we see the work of a New Testament apostle. He sailed with his crew into new territories where they began to colonize and construct the life, language, and culture of the Church. This included all the infrastructure needed for the Body of Christ to function and flourish in the new region. When they were finished, they reboarded their ship and hit the high seas to do it again.

Number Two: An apostle was also like a travel document or a passport that enabled the apostle and his team to journey into new geographical areas to preach the Gospel, to drive back darkness, and to replicate the life, language, and culture of the Church. Thus, an apostle has a door-opening anointing on his life.

Number Three: Apostles are also like *a spiritual package* that is packed with God's powerful anointing to do whatever is needed onsite. He is also a spiritual messenger from God who is gifted with special insight and revelation and whose function is to lead others upward into new spiritual realms and dimensions.

Number Four: Additionally, an apostle was — and is — *an ambassador* who represented Christ in the same way an ambassador would represent a king or government. He served as a tried and tested emissary, messenger, governmental agent, high-ranking diplomat, or as we have seen, an ambassador. Apostles are hand-chosen, powerful individuals who have the spiritual clout and the backing of Heaven to fulfill any assignment that God ever gives them.

Now, while this information may be new to you, it was not new to the ears of New Testament believers. As a result of growing up in a Greek-speaking world, they had heard the word *apostolos* many times and, therefore, they already knew and understood all of these nuances and meanings as well as how they overlapped with each other. That is probably why the apostle Paul never stopped to elaborate on or explain the meaning of an apostle to early believers.

In Lesson 6, we will take a close look at how many apostles are actually named in the New Testament. If you think this list includes only the original Twelve selected by Jesus at the onset of His ministry, you are in for a surprise.

STUDY QUESTIONS

> Study to shew thyself approved unto God, a workman that
> needeth not to be ashamed, rightly dividing the word of truth.
> — 2 Timothy 2:15

1. Although apostles hold an elevated rank as dignitaries in the Church, we also have a very important role to play. According to Second Corinthians 5:17 and 18, to what ministry have we been called? What does God desire to do through you in this ministry (*see* 2 Corinthians 5:19,20)?

2. Receiving understanding and revelation from God is a priceless blessing given to every believer, but not every Christian is a recipient of

this blessing. What does the Bible say we need to do to receive God's wisdom and revelation?

- **Proverbs 1:7; Proverbs 9:10; Psalm 111:10**
- **Psalm 25:8,9; Psalm 25:12-14**
- **First Corinthians 2:9,10; John 16:13-15**
- **James 1:5-7**

PRACTICAL APPLICATION

> But be ye doers of the word, and not hearers only,
> deceiving your own selves.
> —James 1:22

1. Take a moment to reread the section titled "Understanding the Role of Ambassadors in the Ancient World" in this lesson. How does this help you better understand the role of apostles in the Church?
2. By hanging onto Paul's apostolic coattails and being in partnership with him, many churches heard amazing truths that others didn't have access to. Who has God called you to support and partner with in ministry? Have you obeyed His direction? If so, how is the anointing on that minister's life affecting you? If not, what is keeping you from obeying God?

LESSON 6

TOPIC

How Many People Does the New Testament Identify as Apostles?

SCRIPTURES

1. **Hebrew 3:1** — Wherefore, holy brethren, partakers of the heavenly calling, consider the Apostle and High Priest of our profession, Christ Jesus.

2. **Revelation 21:14** — And the wall of the city had twelve foundations, and in them the names of the twelve apostles of the Lamb.
3. **Matthew 10:1-4** — And when he had called unto him his twelve disciples, he gave them power against unclean spirits, to cast them out, and to heal all manner of sickness and all manner of disease. Now the names of the twelve apostles are these; the first, Simon, who is called Peter, and Andrew his brother; James the son of Zebedee, and John his brother; Philip, and Bartholomew; Thomas, and Matthew the publican; James the son of Alphaeus, and Lebbaeus, whose surname was Thaddaeus; Simon the Canaanite, and Judas Iscariot, who also betrayed him.
4. **Luke 6:13** — And when it was day, he called unto him his disciples: and of them he chose twelve, whom also he named apostles.
5. **Acts 1:24-26** — And they prayed, and said, Thou, Lord, which knowest the hearts of all men, shew whether of these two thou hast chosen, that he may take part of this ministry and apostleship, from which Judas by transgression fell, that he might go to his own place. And they gave forth their lots; and the lot fell upon Matthias; and he was numbered with the eleven apostles.
6. **Ephesians 4:11-13** — And he gave some, apostles; and some, prophets; and some, evangelists; and some, pastors and teachers; for the perfecting of the saints, for the work of the ministry, for the edifying of the body of Christ: till we all come in the unity of the faith, and of the knowledge of the Son of God, unto a perfect man, unto the measure of the stature of the fulness of Christ.

SYNOPSIS

How many apostles are mentioned in the New Testament? If you guessed 12, you are in good company. Many people think the only apostles in the New Testament were the 12 original apostles selected by Jesus who served with Him and carried on His ministry. A few people will add in the apostle Paul, bringing the number to 13. But is that accurate? Are there only 12 or 13 apostles mentioned in Scripture? The answer to this question may surprise you, and that is the focus of this lesson.

The emphasis of this lesson:

Along with Jesus Christ — the Chief Apostle of the Church — the New Testament mentions more than two dozen individuals who served as

apostles. Church leaders in Ephesus even created criteria to verify who was a true apostle, and these standards can still be applied to those who claim to be apostles today.

Jesus Was the First Apostle

Have you ever stopped to think about who the first apostle was? The Bible actually reveals this fact in Hebrews 3:1, which states, "Wherefore, holy brethren, partakers of the heavenly calling, consider the Apostle and High Priest of our profession, Christ Jesus."

In this verse, the word "apostle" is the Greek word *apostolos*, and it is used to describe Jesus as the Chief Apostle of the Church. It is He who set the standard for all apostles who would follow Him, and if we are true to Scripture, we will see that Jesus fulfilled every aspect of the meaning of the word "apostle." Consider this:

- **Jesus was God's Admiral.** He went into new territory where the Kingdom of God had never before existed, and with the help of His specialized, apostolic crew (the disciples), He brought Heaven to earth.

- **Jesus was God's Passport.** He brought the disciples and countless others into deep spiritual dimensions they could have never gone to on their own.

- **Jesus was God's Special Package and God's Special Messenger.** Without question, He carried within Himself unprecedented supernatural insights and power given to Him by the Father that were vital for the growth and the building up of the Church.

- **Jesus was, and is, God's Ambassador.** He is backed by all of Heaven, He is equipped with all power and all authority, and He is authorized to speak and act on God's behalf.

Thus, Jesus was the first Apostle of the Church, and as such, He selected and personally trained a team of 12 men to be a part of His apostolic crew. These men each carried on the work of Jesus after His ascension into Heaven and were instrumental in seeing the Church exponentially expand.

Who Were the Original 12 Apostles?

Choosing the Twelve was one of the most important decisions Jesus had to make. To get direction from the Father, the Bible says, "…He went out into a mountain to pray, and continued all night in prayer to God. And when it was day, he called unto him his disciples: and of them he chose twelve, whom also he named apostles" (Luke 6:12,13).

One of the most detailed lists of the 12 men Jesus chose to be apostles is found in **Matthew 10:1-4**. Here Matthew wrote:

> **And when he had called unto him his twelve disciples, he gave them power against unclean spirits, to cast them out, and to heal all manner of sickness and all manner of disease. Now the names of the twelve apostles are these; the first, Simon, who is called Peter, and Andrew his brother; James the son of Zebedee, and John his brother; Philip, and Bartholomew; Thomas, and Matthew the publican; James the son of Alphaeus, and Lebbaeus, whose surname was Thaddaeus; Simon the Canaanite, and Judas Iscariot, who also betrayed him.**

These 12 men are what Rick calls *foundational apostles*. Next to Jesus, they sacrificially gave their lives to build the Church and were moved on by the Holy Spirit to write doctrinal truths of the Christian faith that are nonnegotiable. Interestingly, the apostle John referred to the original apostles as "the twelve apostles of the Lamb" (Revelation 21:14). Clearly, there will never be another group of apostles like these.

A Replacement for Judas

Of the original 12 apostles, we know that Judas Iscariot betrayed Jesus and went out afterward and committed suicide because he couldn't live with what he had done. The Bible records that after Jesus died, was resurrected, and ascended into Heaven, His devout followers returned to the upper room in Jerusalem where they were told to wait for the empowerment of the Holy Spirit (*see* Luke 24:49).

While they waited, the disciples took to the business of choosing a replacement for Judas. The Scripture says, "And they prayed, and said, Thou, Lord, which knowest the hearts of all men, shew whether of these two thou hast chosen, that he may take part of this ministry and apostleship, from which Judas by transgression fell, that he might go to his own place. And they gave forth their lots; and the lot fell upon Matthias; and he was numbered with the eleven apostles" (Acts 1:24-26).

In these three verses, a form of the word "apostle" — the Greek word *apostolos* — appears twice. Matthias was selected to be numbered with the remaining apostles. So, if we count everyone who has been called an *apostolos* up to now — including Jesus as the first Apostle — the number of apostles mentioned in the New Testament so far is 14. This includes the original 12, Jesus, and Matthias, Judas' replacement.

What Other Apostles Are Named in the New Testament?

To the surprise of many, there are numerous other apostles we read about in the Scriptures. Hence, the word "apostle" is used in a broader sense. In addition to the 14 we've mentioned, here is a list of bona fide, biblical apostles and where they are mentioned in the Bible:

- **Paul,** who called himself an apostle at the opening of many of his letters (Romans 1:1; 1 Corinthians 1:1; 2 Corinthians 1:1; Galatians 1:1; Ephesians 1:1; Colossians 1:1)
- **Barnabas** (Acts 13:2,3,50; 14:14; 1 Corinthians 9:5,6)
- **Apollos** (1 Corinthians 4:6-13)
- **Epaphroditus,** here *apostolos* is translated as "messenger" (Philippians 2:25)
- **Andronicus,** a relative of Paul (Romans 16:7)
- **Junia,** the wife of Andronicus (Romans 16:7)
- **Titus,** here *apostolos* is translated as "messenger" (2 Corinthians 8:23)
- **An unnamed brother** with Titus (2 Corinthians 8:16-23)
- **Another unnamed brother** with Titus (2 Corinthians 8:22,23)
- **Timothy** (1 Thessalonians 1:1; 2:6)
- **Silvanus or Silas** (1 Thessalonians 1:1; 2:6)
- **James,** the half-brother of Jesus (Galatians 1:19)

If we count all those in the New Testament to whom the word *apostolos* is specifically applied, there are at least 26 people who were described as apostles and who did apostolic work. We say "at least" 26 because there are actually a few more we could potentially add to the list.

These additional apostles are certainly not in the same category as the foundational apostles; nevertheless, they were Christ-given apostles in a broader sense of the word who helped establish the Church in conjunction with the other fivefold ministry gifts.

This means that contrary to what many denominations teach, real apostolic ministry is not limited to the original 12 apostles, nor did this Christ-given fivefold ministry gift cease with the close of the Apostolic Age.

'Apostleship' Is One of the Fivefold Ministry Gifts

As we've noted in previous lessons, the office of an apostle is one of the fivefold ministry gifts Jesus gave to the Church. Paul named all five gifts in Ephesians 4:11-13:

> And he [Jesus] gave some, apostles; and some, prophets; and some, evangelists; and some, pastors and teachers; for the perfecting of the saints, for the work of the ministry, for the edifying of the body of Christ: till we all come in the unity of the faith, and of the knowledge of the Son of God, unto a perfect man, unto the measure of the stature of the fulness of Christ.

Notice the purpose for which Christ gave us these gifts — for the perfecting of the saints, for the work of ministry, and for the edifying (or building up) of the Body of Christ (v. 12). How long will all five of these gifts — including the ministry of apostles and prophets — be actively at work in the Church? The Bible says, "Till we all come in the unity of the faith, and of the knowledge of the Son of God, unto a perfect man, unto the measure of the stature of the fulness of Christ" (v. 13).

The Church of Ephesus Created Criterion to Verify True Apostles

It should be noted that the Early Church never questioned that there could be other apostles in addition to the original group that Jesus chose.

They knew this was an essential fivefold ministry gift that extended beyond the foundational apostles.

In fact, by the end of the First Century, there were so many people claiming to be apostles that the church of Ephesus decided to develop criteria based on Scripture to help determine who was and who wasn't a real apostle. These efforts by the leadership of the church at Ephesus were so imperative and so outstanding that Jesus commended them for it in Revelation 2:2, where He said:

> **I know thy works, and thy labour, and thy patience, and how thou canst not bear them which are evil: and thou hast tried them which say they are apostles, and are not....**

Jesus pointed out the fact that the church of Ephesus "tried" the people who said they were apostles. This word "tried" is from the Greek word *peiradzo*, which was used to describe *the fiery process of testing and removing impurities from metal*. It also denoted *the process of testing coins to determine if they were real or counterfeit*.

With the inundation of individuals alleging to be apostles, church leaders at Ephesus began vigorously vetting anyone who was making such a claim. As much as possible, they wanted to spare the church from the assault of pretenders by weeding them out before they had an opportunity to inflict damage. This testing also served to protect the reputation of the real apostles, which was put at risk by all the false apostles.

Keep in mind that the church in Ephesus was birthed in the supernatural power of God and was marked by true, bona fide apostolic ministry. Thus, they were very familiar with the signs that should accompany real apostles. It's likely the leaders at Ephesus borrowed the standards established by Peter and the other apostles when they selected candidates for Judas' replacement. These were:

1. **The person had to have personally seen Jesus' ministry with his own eyes.**

2. **The person had to have personally witnessed Jesus' resurrection.**

Matthias met these qualifications, and that's why he was chosen to be the replacement for Judas Iscariot.

The apostle Paul took it a step further and added other criteria. In fact, he included six biblical proofs of apostleship, and if a person doesn't meet all six of them, he is not an apostle. This will be the focus of our next lesson.

STUDY QUESTIONS

> Study to shew thyself approved unto God, a workman that needeth not to be ashamed, rightly dividing the word of truth.
> —2 Timothy 2:15

1. Carefully read Matthew 10:1-4; Mark 3:13-19; along with Luke 6:12-16 and list the 12 foundational apostles Jesus chose to carry on His ministry. What stands out to you about how these men are described (i.e., their relation to each other, their occupation, etc.)?
2. John also records the calling of several of the apostles in John 1:35-51. How is his description different than that of Matthew, Mark, and Luke?
3. In your own words, describe the criteria that was first used by the Early Church to determine if a person was — or was not — a genuine apostle (*see* Acts 1:21,22). Why do you think these standards were so important at that time?

PRACTICAL APPLICATION

> But be ye doers of the word, and not hearers only, deceiving your own selves.
> —James 1:22

1. Have you ever thought of Jesus as the first and Chief Apostle of the Church? How does this fact expand your understanding of His ministry and who He is?
2. Were you surprised to learn that there are more than two dozen apostles mentioned in Scripture? What about this detailed list of apostles documented by Paul is most interesting to you? Why?

LESSON 7

TOPIC
What Are the Authenticating Signs of a Genuine Apostle? Part 1

SCRIPTURES
1. **Revelation 2:2** — I know thy works, and thy labor, and thy patience, and how thou canst not bear them which are evil: and thou hast tried them which say they are apostles, and are not....
2. **1 Corinthians 9:1** — Am I not an apostle? am I not free? have I not seen Jesus Christ our Lord? are not ye my work in the Lord?

SYNOPSIS
In recent years, it seems that more and more people are labeling themselves as an *apostle* or a *prophet* of the Lord, but many of these individuals are not apostles or prophets at all. Although some are purposely insincere, most people making this mistake are simply misinformed. Due to a lack of solid teaching in this area, they have misinterpreted their apostolic or prophetic leaning as being equal to being called by Christ into one of these fivefold ministry gifts.

This phenomenon is actually not new. A similar situation was taking place in the Early Church. The number of people claiming to be apostles was so great that Church leaders had to create a criteria to confirm who was and was not an apostle. So, who was it that developed this test, and what are the authenticating signs that confirm a person is a genuine apostle?

The emphasis of this lesson:

In addition to the criteria developed by the leaders of the church of Ephesus, the apostle Paul added six significant proofs to confirm whether or not a person is truly an apostle. These are found in First Corinthians 9:1 and Second Corinthians 12:12.

The Church of Ephesus Took the Role of Apostleship Seriously

As we noted in Lesson 6, there were so many people professing to be apostles toward the end of the First Century that the Ephesian believers developed criteria to determine the veracity of their claims. The church in Ephesus had been born in the supernatural power of God and true apostolic ministry. They had a strong relationship with the apostle Paul and other apostles, and therefore, they were very familiar with the signs that accompanied bona fide apostles.

Jesus even commended the leaders of Ephesus for their diligence in developing a test to verify who was and wasn't a genuine apostle. He said:

> **I know thy works, and thy labour, and thy patience, and how thou canst not bear them which are evil: and thou hast tried them which say they are apostles, and are not, and hast found them liars.**
>
> — **Revelation 2:2**

The word "tried" in this passage is a translation of the Greek word *peiradzo*, which was used to describe *the fiery process of testing and removing impurities from metal* as well as *the process of testing coins to determine if they were real or counterfeit*. When individuals came to Ephesus boasting of being an apostle, the leadership put their character to the test. According to this verse, many of these individuals failed the test and were "found" to be liars.

The word "found" used here is from the Greek word *heurisko*, and it primarily means *to discover as a result of an intense investigation*. It is from where we get the word *eureka*. The use of this word tells us that the church of Ephesus conducted a thorough investigation of each person alleging to be an apostle, and from their diligent search, they exposed many who had been masterfully masquerading as apostles but were fakes.

It should also be noted that the church of Ephesus was the largest church in the region, and as such, it became the training center for countless Christians who were launched out into ministry in other areas of Asia. The believers in Ephesus understood they were accountable to God for endorsing ministers. If they made an error in their judgment of a person and then sent them out, their error would affect the other developing churches.

Thus, the leaders refused to be swayed or hoodwinked by outward appearances. They believed the issue of apostolic ministry was so vital and needed in the development of the Church that they did all that was within their power to examine people who claimed to be apostles in order to protect and honor the office and not let it be tarnished by false apostles.

Three Proofs of a Genuine Apostle

The apostle Paul took the idea of testing the genuineness of people's claims to a whole new level, developing six biblical proofs of apostleship. Let's look at the first three of these proofs and see how they still apply to apostles in the Church today.

Proof Number 1: An Apostle Is Marked by a Supernatural Vision of Jesus

In our last lesson, we saw that the first criterion to being an apostle was developed by the 11 remaining foundational apostles who were looking for a replacement for Judas Iscariot. They believed that to be an apostle one had to have personally seen Jesus' ministry with his own eyes and to have personally witnessed His resurrection (*see* Acts 1:15-26).

In addition to these supernatural visions, Paul added criteria, which he wrote about in First Corinthians 9:1. In defense of his apostleship, he said, "Am I not an apostle? am I not free? have I not seen Jesus Christ our Lord? are not ye my work in the Lord?"

Now you may be thinking, *When did Paul see the Lord? He must have seen Him for him to make such a bold statement.* Well, it is certainly possible that Paul physically saw Jesus during one of Christ's many visits to the city of Jerusalem since they were both about the same age. Although there is no biblical or historical proof to validate this, it is not out of the question.

However, Paul was not alluding to this. Rather, he was talking about personally seeing Jesus, beginning with his encounter on the road to Damascus when he surrendered his life to Christ and first called Him Lord (*see* Acts 9:1-6). Other encounters and conversations with Jesus ensued after this, which we know from Jesus' own words in Acts 26:16. He told Paul that He had made him "…a minister and a witness both of these things which thou hast seen, and *of those things in the which I will appear unto thee.*"

So, based on Jesus' words, we know Paul had seen Him in multiple visions and received divine insights and revelation regarding the Gospel, Christ Himself, and the Body of Christ. Paul believed these visions qualified him to meet the first criterion for being a true apostle, which is to have personally seen the risen Christ.

To effectively build the Church, Paul was given a clear apostolic vision of it. Remember, the Church is the Body of Christ — and this vision perhaps also qualified as Paul "seeing" the Lord. One thing is sure: For an apostle to do his work, he must have a clear understanding and vision of Christ and His lordship and headship in the Church.

Today, there are people called to apostolic work who have never had a literal vision of Jesus Himself, but they have had, and have, a burning vision of Christ in His Church that compels them to do what they do. This is what qualifies them to be a modern-day apostle.

So, **proof number 1** is: *Has this individual who claims to be an apostle seen the risen Christ? If they have not, do they really have a bona fide, burning vision in them of Christ in the Church?*

Proof Number 2: An Apostle Is Marked With Supernaturally Proven Fruit

Looking again at Paul's words regarding his apostleship, he said, "Am I not an apostle? am I not free? have I not seen Jesus Christ our Lord? are not ye my work in the Lord?" (1 Corinthians 9:1). In this passage, Paul was speaking to the entire church of Corinth, and he was pointing to the churches he had started — including the church of Corinth — as proof that he was indeed an apostle.

The Greek word for "apostle" here is again *apostolos*, the word we have been examining for several lessons, and it is important to note that this term is never used in the New Testament except to describe those who start and lead churches.

Pointing to the churches he had started as proof of his apostleship, Paul made it clear that if a person has *not* started churches, *plural*, he simply does not qualify to be called an apostle — *period*. If an individual has not driven back the forces of hell and planted churches where the Church in those localities previously did not exist, he simply does not scripturally qualify to be called an apostle.

Even today, if a person has no record of ever starting churches or leading churches, he is categorically not an apostle. Although he may be blessed with supernatural activity and wonderful insights, the fact that he has not started or led churches means he simply does not qualify as an apostle.

So, **proof number 2** is: *Does the individual before us, who claims to be an apostle, have the proven track record and fruit of churches he has started and leads?*

Proof Number 3: An Apostle Is Marked With Supernatural Patience

We saw in an earlier lesson that the first authenticating sign of apostleship Paul gave is having *patience*. We find this truth in Second Corinthians 12:12 where Paul wrote, "Truly the signs of an apostle were wrought among you in all patience, in signs, and wonders, and mighty deeds." Although signs, wonders, and mighty deeds are what many people immediately gravitate toward as signs of an apostle, it is actually "patience" that is most important.

Anyone involved in doing apostolic work understands this. Being able to do the will of God and to stay in the will of God in the face of hell is just as significant as signs and wonders and mighty deeds. In fact, it may be even more important, and that is why Paul lists it first in this verse.

Paul said, "Truly the signs of an apostle were wrought among you in all patience…" (2 Corinthians 12:12). The opening word "truly" is the equivalent of Paul saying, *"Certainly, emphatically, most definitely…."* Patience is required for a person to be an apostle — to serve on the front lines of spiritual warfare and fight against the powers of darkness and bulldoze demonic opposition so that the Kingdom of God may be established and advance in places it has never existed.

This word "patience" is the Greek word *hupomene*, which is a compound of the words *hupo*, meaning *to be under*, and *meno*, which depicts *a determination to stay in one's place*. When these words are compounded to form *hupomene*, it describes *the ability to stay or abide or to remain in one's spot*. It means *to keep a position or to resolve to maintain territory gained*. In a military sense, it pictures soldiers ordered to maintain their positions even in the face of opposition.

Those who are called of God to apostolic work are often assigned to areas that are not for the faint of heart. To remain at their post and to not cave in to the pressures and attacks of the enemy, *patience* is needed. *Hupomene* — the Greek word for "patience" — carries the idea of *defiantly sticking it out regardless of pressures mounted against it*. It is *staying power, hang-in-there power*, and *the attitude that holds out, holds on, outlasts, perseveres, and hangs in there, never giving up, refusing to surrender to obstacles and turning down every opportunity to quit*. A person operating in "patience" is one who is under a heavy load but refuses to bend, break, or surrender because he is convinced that the territory, promise, or principle under assault rightfully belongs to him.

So, **proof number 3** is: *Does this person who calls himself an apostle demonstrate supernatural endurance in his life? Or does he tuck his tail and run when times get tough?* Once a genuine apostle has walked through an open door, he is anointed to stay there even if that open door comes with hostile adversaries.

In our next lesson, we will examine three more proofs Paul gave us to verify whether or not a person is truly an apostle.

STUDY QUESTIONS

> **Study to shew thyself approved unto God, a workman that needeth not to be ashamed, rightly dividing the word of truth.**
> — 2 Timothy 2:15

The church of Ephesus knew they were accountable to God for who they endorsed as an apostle. Thus, they refused to be swayed or hoodwinked by outward appearances.

1. What does this say to you personally about the decisions (and endorsements) *you* make regarding the character and spiritual maturity of others?
2. What can you learn from Isaiah 11:2 and 3 about making an accurate assessment of a person's character?
3. Also consider Jesus' words in John 7:2-24 and God's words to Samuel in First Samuel 16:3-13, regarding the selection of David to be the

next king. What do these passages tell you about making a judgment call strictly on what you see?

PRACTICAL APPLICATION

> But be ye doers of the word, and not hearers only, deceiving your own selves.
> —James 1:22

1. One of the primary signs of an authentic apostle is supernatural patience — *staying power, hang-in-there power,* and *the attitude that holds out, holds on, outlasts, perseveres, and hangs in there, never giving up, refusing to surrender to obstacles and turning down every opportunity to quit.* Have you ever experienced a situation when this divine empowerment was operating in your life?
2. If the answer is yes, how did you know it was happening? What were the immediate, tangible results you experienced?
3. Do you need supernatural endurance for what you're currently walking through? Take time to reflect on Isaiah 40:28-31 and ask the Holy Spirit to cultivate His strength in you to outlast the enemy and receive God's promised blessings.

LESSON 8

TOPIC

What Are the Authenticating Signs of a Genuine Apostle? Part 2

SCRIPTURES

1. **2 Corinthians 12:12** — Truly the signs of an apostle were wrought among you in all patience, in signs, and wonders, and mighty deeds.
2. **Acts 28:3,5,6** — And when Paul had gathered a bundle of sticks, and laid them on the fire, there came a viper out of the heat, and fastened on his hand. ... And he shook off the beast into the fire, and felt no harm. Howbeit they looked when he should have swollen, or fallen down dead suddenly: but after they had looked a great while, and saw

no harm come to him, they changed their minds, and said that he was a god.

3. **Acts 16:24-26** — Who, having received such a charge, thrust them [Paul and Silas] into the inner prison, and made their feet fast in the stocks. And at midnight Paul and Silas prayed, and sang praises unto God: and the prisoners heard them. And suddenly there was a great earthquake, so that the foundations of the prison were shaken: and immediately all the doors were opened, and every one's bands were loosed.

GREEK WORDS

1. "truly" — τὰ μὲν (*ta men*): emphatically or indeed; it could be translated, "of a certainty!"
2. "signs" — σημεῖον (*semeion*): an announcement, guarantee, or proof
3. "patience" — ὑπομονή (*hupomene*): to stay or abide; to remain in one's spot; to keep a position; to resolve to maintain territory gained; in a military sense, it pictures soldiers ordered to maintain their positions even in the face of opposition; to defiantly stick it out regardless of pressures mounted against it; staying power; hang-in-there power; the attitude that holds out, holds on, outlasts, perseveres, and hangs in there, never giving up, refusing to surrender to obstacles, and turning down every opportunity to quit; it pictures one who is under a heavy load but refuses to bend, break, or surrender because he is convinced that the territory, promise, or principle under assault rightfully belongs to him
4. "wonders" — τέρας (*teras*): an event that leaves one baffled, bewildered, or astonished; depicts the shock, surprise, or astonishment felt by bystanders who observe events that were contrary to the normal course of nature; such events were viewed as miracles, and people believed they could only take place through the intervention of divine power
5. "mighty deeds" — δύναμις (*dunamis*): explosive, superhuman power that comes with enormous energy and produces phenomenal, extraordinary, and unparalleled results; also the word for a force of nature, like a hurricane, tornado, or earthquake; depicts "mighty deeds" that are impressive, incomparable, and beyond human ability to perform — denoting events that, like a spiritual hurricane, tornado, or earthquake, really shake people up and leave them reeling in their minds

SYNOPSIS

In our last lesson, we outlined three biblical proofs that authenticate whether a person is a bona fide apostle or not. The apostle Paul established these proofs in his two letters to the church of Corinth.

Proof #1: If a person is a real apostle, he will be marked with a supernatural vision of Jesus or of Christ in the Church.

Proof #2: If a person is truly an apostle, he will be marked with supernaturally proven fruit. Remember, an apostle is like an admiral who, with his apostolic crew, sails into virgin territory to establish the Church where it's never been established before. Hence, a proof that one is an apostle is that they have started churches (plural) and are leading churches.

Proof #3: If a person is really an apostle, he will be marked with *supernatural patience*. Paul said, "Truly the signs of an apostle were wrought among you in all patience…" (2 Corinthians 12:12). In Greek, the word "patience" is *hupomene*, which would be better translated as *supernatural endurance*. It is the power to stay put and not abandon ship when things get difficult.

To list patience as a supernatural sign may seem strange, but anyone who understands genuine apostolic ministry knows that it often takes place in very difficult and uncomfortable conditions. It is frontline ministry — it is like a spiritual military expedition to push into new territory, to fight against the powers of darkness, and then to bulldoze demonic opposition out of the way so the foundation of the Church can be established where it never existed before.

Only a dose of this supernatural endurance can give sufficient strength to an apostle to keep pressing forward when it seems all of hell is raging against him. Individuals with a real apostolic call live on the frontlines and do frontline work in environments that are difficult and often hostile to the Gospel.

The emphasis of this lesson:

Three additional proofs Paul gave that demonstrate a person is truly an apostle include the working of supernatural signs, divine wonders, and mighty deeds. These proofs, along with the others, are meant to encourage people to accurately discern who is a real apostle and who is a fake.

Proof Number 4: Supernatural 'Signs'

The fourth proof the Bible gives confirming a person is indeed an apostle is the demonstration of "signs." Paul wrote, "Truly the signs of an apostle were wrought among you in all patience, [and] in signs…" (2 Corinthians 12:12). The word "truly" in Greek is *ta men*, which means *emphatically* or *indeed*, and it could be translated *"of a certainty!"* The word "signs" is a translation of the Greek word *semeion*, and it describes *an announcement, guarantee, or proof*. It is *an authenticating marker* clearly demonstrating — in this case — that an apostle truly is an apostle.

Now some people believe Paul's ministry was a continual series of one supernatural sign after another. However, if you examine the book of Acts to determine the regularity of supernatural signs, you will find they did not occur nonstop as you might have expected. On the contrary, signs and wonders occurred at pivotal and crucial moments when miracles were needed to open the door for the Gospel even wider.

Consider these authenticating signs of Paul's apostleship documented in the book of Acts:

- In the city of Lystra, strength was suddenly restored to the limbs of a man who was lame from birth (Acts 14:8-10).

- In Philippi, demons were cast out of a woman who was a fortuneteller (Acts 16:16-18).

- In Ephesus, many people couldn't make it to the meetings to hear Paul preach, so handkerchiefs, aprons, and clothing that had touched Paul's anointed body were taken and placed on individuals who were sick and bedridden. God's healing power was transferred from the garments to those with diseases, and they were healed and set free from demonic influence (Acts 19:11,12).

- In Troas, a young man that fell out of a window and died was raised from the dead (Acts 20:9-12).

- On the island of Melita, when Paul was stranded, several people who were sick received supernatural healing through Paul (Acts 28:8,9).

In all these cities, supernatural signs accompanied Paul, serving as divine proof that he was indeed an apostle, and they opened a massive door of opportunity for the Gospel to be proclaimed. Again, these signs didn't occur all at once, but at pivotal moments in Paul's ministry when they made the greatest impact.

Thus, an apostle's ministry is marked with supernatural signs. With this understanding, leaders in the Early Church grew accustomed to asking the question, *Has the individual who claims to be an apostle had miraculous signs at pivotal moments in his ministry?*

Proof Number 5: Supernatural 'Wonders'

What other evidence does the Bible say authenticates whether a person is indeed an apostle? Second Corinthians 12:12 says, "Truly the signs of an apostle were wrought among you in all patience, in signs, and wonders…." Now, you may be thinking, *What's the difference between signs and wonders?*

The word "wonders" in this verse is a form of the Greek word *teras*, which describes *an event that leaves one baffled, bewildered, or astonished*. It depicts the *shock, surprise,* or *astonishment felt by bystanders who observe events that are contrary to the normal course of nature.* Such events were viewed as miracles, and people believed they could only take place through the intervention of divine power.

This tells us that when an individual has an authentic apostolic calling on his life, there will be moments in his ministry when baffling "wonders" take place. That is what took place when Paul was shipwrecked on the island of Melita. The Bible says that as he was gathering wood for the fire, "…There came a viper out of the heat, and fastened on his hand. And when the barbarians saw the venomous beast hang on his hand, they said among themselves, No doubt this man is a murderer, whom, though he hath escaped the sea, yet vengeance suffereth not to live" (Acts 28:3,4).

Much to their amazement, Paul "…shook off the beast into the fire, and felt no harm" (Acts 28:5). God's power intervened and negated the effects of the venom. This "wonder" had such an impact on the island people that they changed their view of Paul and believed he was a god, which opened their hearts to hear the Gospel message.

With this proof in mind, many believers began to ask the question, *Has the individual who claims to be an apostle had supernatural wonders in his ministry?*

Proof Number 6: An Apostle Is Marked With 'Mighty Deeds'

Along with supernatural signs and wonders, the Bible says "mighty deeds" are a sign of a true apostle. "Truly the signs of an apostle were wrought among you in all patience, in signs, and wonders, *and* mighty deeds" (2 Corinthians 12:12). Interestingly, when we read this portion of Scripture in the original Greek, the word "and" is the word *kai*, which could be translated as *even*. It is the equivalent of Paul saying, "*Even* mighty deeds are a sign of an apostle."

This brings us to the phrase "mighty deeds," which is a translation of the Greek word *dunamis*. This remarkable word describes *explosive, superhuman power that comes with enormous energy and produces phenomenal, extraordinary, and unparalleled results.* The word *dunamis* is the term Jesus used to depict the power of the Holy Spirit that filled the believers gathered in the upper room on the Day of Pentecost. This word was also used by the ancient Greeks to describe *a force of nature* like a *hurricane, tornado,* or *earthquake.*

Thus, the words "mighty deeds" depict actions and events that are impressive, incomparable, and beyond human ability to perform. They denote events that, like a spiritual hurricane, tornado, or earthquake, really shake people up and leave them reeling in their minds. The use of this word tells us emphatically that when the supernatural power of God is manifesting through an apostle, the laws of nature are suspended or overruled.

One of the best examples of "mighty deeds" manifesting is when Paul and Silas were beaten and thrown in jail for preaching the Gospel in the city of Philippi. The Bible says that the authorities "…thrust them into the inner prison, and made their feet fast in the stocks. And at midnight Paul and Silas prayed, and sang praises unto God: and the prisoners heard them. And suddenly there was a great earthquake, so that the foundations of the prison were shaken: and immediately all the doors were opened, and every one's bands were loosed" (Acts 16:24-26).

Imagine that — out of nowhere, an earthquake took place and violently shook only the prison! And this quake was so unique that it opened all the prison doors and broke the chains off all the prisoners, making a way for Paul and Silas to go free. Wow! Can you say, "mighty deeds"? That is exactly what this supernatural phenomenon was, and when people heard the news of the event, it left them in a state of shock and wonder. Indeed, they were astonished, bewildered, and left speechless by what took place.

Now there's one more thing worth noting about this word *dunamis* — which is translated here as "mighty deeds." It was also used to depict *the full advancing force of a mighty army that drives back enemies and takes new territory*. This lets us know that part of the "mighty deeds" Paul was referring to in this verse was the forceful advancement of the Gospel in dark and hostile locations where it would have naturally been impossible to do God's work.

So, when God's power operates in and through apostles, they're able to drive back the powers of hell, bulldoze all demonic activity out of the way, and establish the Church where it's never been established before. With this knowledge, leaders in the Early Church developed the habit of asking the question, *"Has the individual who claims to be an apostle experienced mighty deeds at pivotal moments in his ministry?"*

A Review of the Six Proofs of Apostleship

Again, to deal with the large number of people who were claiming to be apostles in the First Century, the Early Church developed criteria to determine who was and who was not an authentic, New Testament apostle. Here are the six proofs they used to test and confirm a person's apostleship:

> **Proof 1:** Has this person had a vision of Jesus or of Christ in the Church?
>
> **Proof 2:** Does this person have the supernatural fruit of having started multiple churches?
>
> **Proof 3:** Does this person have supernatural patience to stay put? Does he or she have divine endurance?
>
> **Proof 4:** Is this person's ministry marked with supernatural signs?
>
> **Proof 5:** Is this person's ministry marked with supernatural wonders?
>
> **Proof 6:** Is this person's ministry marked with mighty deeds?

To be clear, theses proofs were not intended to promote suspicion, but rather, to encourage discernment — exposing those who were fake and protecting those with real Christ-given apostolic gifts. The apostolic call is vital for building up the local church, and those who imitate this call for the sake of personal gain should not be tolerated. If a person has an authentic apostolic call, a test or a little scrutiny won't hurt or diminish it. It will only prove that the call is genuine.

In our next lesson, we'll dig a bit deeper and discover why someone would claim to be an apostle if he really wasn't one.

STUDY QUESTIONS

> Study to shew thyself approved unto God, a workman that needeth not to be ashamed, rightly dividing the word of truth.
> — 2 Timothy 2:15

1. Prior to this lesson, did you think supernatural signs and wonders were constantly happening in Paul's ministry? How does the fact that signs and wonders only took place at pivotal or crucial moments change your perspective of his ministry?
2. At first glance, someone may think that supernatural "signs," "wonders," and "mighty deeds" are all the same, but they are not. In your own words, describe the differences between these three proofs of an apostle.
3. Out of all the signs, wonders, and mighty deeds recorded in the New Testament, name one that has left you truly amazed. Why is this apostolic manifestation so impactful to you?

PRACTICAL APPLICATION

> But be ye doers of the word, and not hearers only, deceiving your own selves.
> — James 1:22

1. One of the most fascinating signs that accompanied Paul is recorded in Acts 19:11 and 12, when handkerchiefs, aprons, and clothing that had touched his anointed body were taken and placed on individuals who were sick and bedridden and they were healed. How does this manifestation light a fire of faith in your heart? What does it give you hope to believe for in your own life?

2. Part of the meaning of "mighty deeds" referred to by Paul in Second Corinthians 12:12 is the forceful advancement of the Gospel in dark and hostile locations where it would have naturally been impossible to do God's work. Have you ever personally witnessed these kinds of *mighty deeds* take place through someone's ministry? If so, briefly describe what happened.

LESSON 9

TOPIC

Why Would Anyone Claim To Be an Apostle if He Wasn't an Apostle?

SCRIPTURES

1. **2 Corinthians 10:15,16** — Not boasting of things without our measure, that is, of other men's labours; but having hope, when your faith is increased, that we shall be enlarged by you according to our rule abundantly, to preach the gospel in the regions beyond you, and not to boast in another man's line of things made ready to our hand.
2. **1 Corinthians 9:2** — If I be not an apostle unto others, yet doubtless I am to you....
3. **2 Corinthians 11:13,14** — For such are false apostles, deceitful workers, transforming themselves into the apostles of Christ. And no marvel; for Satan himself is transformed into an angel of light.

GREEK WORDS

1. "doubtless" — indeed; a better translation would be, "indeed, I am to you!"
2. "false apostles" — ψευδαπόστολος (*pseudapostolos*): a compound of ψευδής (*pseudes*) and ἀπόστολος (*apostolos*); the word ψευδής (*pseudes*) carries the idea of any type of falsehood, and it can picture a person who either intentionally or unintentionally projects a false image of himself, someone who walks under some pretense, or one who projects an image that is untrue

3. "deceitful" — δόλιος (*dolios*): used to describe bait that is put on a hook to catch fish; conveys the idea of craftiness, cheating, cunning, dishonesty, fraud, guile, and trickery intended to entrap someone in an act of deception
4. "workers" — ἐργάτης (*ergates*): someone who actively works at what he is doing
5. "transform" — μετασχηματίζω (*metaschematidzo*): to disguise oneself, to deliberately change one's outward appearance, or to masquerade in clothing that depicts a person as different than he really is

SYNOPSIS

Have you ever stopped to think why someone who was not an apostle would claim to be an apostle? Well, in the First Century, those who spoke and read Greek as their native tongue knew that the word "apostle" depicted a position that held enormous authority and that those who carried this title could obtain leverage in the lives of people in the Church. So, some coveted this name and intentionally claimed it in order to gain control and to exhort power over God's people.

Without question, what an apostle said carried great weight within a church as well as within an entire group of churches. Therefore, whoever laid claim to the apostolic title would potentially be able to influence what happened in the lives of many people.

For a genuine Christ-given apostle, this office was a serious responsibility entrusted to him by Jesus that he exercised with fear, prudence, and holiness. But for a person with impure motives, such a position represented an opportunity for all kinds of selfish gain.

The emphasis of this lesson:

The fact is, being an apostle — in New Testament times and today — is relational, territorial, and at times ethnically driven. People who pretend to be apostles but are not are false apostles, and in most cases, they carry out their charade in the hopes of gaining a personal advantage over others.

Three Main Facets of Being an Apostle

It is really no surprise that during the First Century, the apostle Paul was already confronting the issue of false apostles. Specifically, he had to deal with these pretenders because they were after the churches he had established. Oftentimes, false apostles would lay in wait for Paul to leave town, and as soon as he was gone, they would move on the scene like predators attempting to discredit him so they could take over the churches in his apostolic territory. This brings us to a very important realization regarding apostolic ministry: being an apostle is *relational*, *territorial*, and at times *ethnically* driven.

Being an Apostle Is *Relational*

Even though Paul was universally accepted and respected as a great legendary apostle in the Early Church, he was not an apostle to every First Century church. He was only an apostle to those with whom he had an apostolic *relationship*. That is, Paul was an apostle to the churches he had helped start and to those whom he served as a mentor, a teacher, and a father in the faith.

For example, Paul's apostleship was limited to those for whom he bore direct spiritual responsibility and with whom he had a unique relationship. Hence, Paul was an apostle to the churches of Ephesus, Colossae, Corinth, Galatia, Hierapolis, Laodicea, Pergamum, Philadelphia, Philippi, Sardis, Smyrna, Thyatira, and others. And because he was in relationship with these churches, we have his epistles (or letters) of First and Second Corinthians, Galatians, Ephesians, Philippians, and Colossians.

Being an Apostle Is *Territorial*

One thing about the apostle Paul is that he knew how to stay in his own lane and work the geographic area God entrusted to him. This is confirmed in Second Corinthians 10:15, where Paul said, "Not boasting of things without our measure, that is, of other men's labours...." This is the equivalent of him saying, "We are not boasting of things outside of our territory...."

Paul then added in verse 16 that he and his apostolic crew would preach the Gospel in regions beyond Corinth but "...not to boast in another man's line of things made ready to our hand." This was his way of saying, "We won't take credit for another person's apostolic work."

These two verses let us know that Paul was respectful of the work of other apostles and careful not to trespass into another man's territory and begin working. He was also respectful of the authority Christ had given to others as well as to himself. The last thing Paul wanted to do was create confusion about who was supposed to give direction to certain churches or to whom those churches were accountable.

It's clear from Scripture that Paul knew his place, which explains why in First Corinthians 9:2, he said, "If I be not an apostle unto others, yet doubtless I am to you: for the seal of mine apostleship are ye in the Lord." Again, Paul clearly states here that he is not an apostle to every believer and every church, but he was *indeed* an apostle to the Corinthians. Why? Because he had started the church in Corinth, he had mentored them, and he was like their spiritual father. Clearly, he had an apostolic relationship with the Corinthians.

Being an Apostle Sometimes Relates to a Specific *Ethnic Group*

The Bible tells us that Paul and Peter were called to two different ethnic groups. Peter was called to bring the Gospel to the Jews and was very effective in his efforts. When he tried to focus on the Gentiles, they didn't want to have anything to do with him. On the flipside, Paul was called by God to be an apostle to the Gentiles. When he turned his attention to the Jews — which he did for the first few years of his ministry — he was ineffective and met with tremendous hostility.

As long as Paul and Peter stayed ministering to the ethnic group God had called them to, they had great success, which demonstrates how sometimes apostleship is ethnically related. Still, Paul frequently had to defend his apostleship because of deceitful workers who were attempting to exert their authority over entire regions of churches that he and other fellow apostles had established. These fraudulent workers used every imaginable method to attract, tempt, lure, entice, and seduce the churches who were under Paul's God-ordained authority away from him and over to themselves.

In Paul's case, these false apostles really couldn't find a legitimate reason to accuse him, so they used slanderous and even senseless accusations to try and discredit him and persuade his churches to leave him and come under their authority instead. This is why Paul began so many of his letters by saying, "Paul, an apostle of Jesus Christ." We find this opening greeting in Romans 1:1; First Corinthians 1:1; Second Corinthians 1:1; Galatians 1:1; Ephesians 1:1; and Colossians 1:1. Again and again, he declared who Jesus said he was — a bona fide apostle of the Lord.

There are only three letters where Paul didn't begin by calling himself an apostle of Jesus Christ, and those were his letter to the Philippians and both letters to the Thessalonians. The reason he didn't speak of his apostleship to these believers is because it was not under assault and he had no need to defend his position.

Today, there are still people in the Church who call themselves apostles who are not apostles. In many of these cases, the motive is not self-gain but a lack of understanding of what a genuine apostle really is, which is why this series of teachings has been created. In the following section, we will take a closer look at what a false apostle is.

What Is a 'False Apostle'?

In Second Corinthians 11:13 and 14, the apostle Paul gave us a little more information on false apostles. He wrote, "For such are false apostles, deceitful workers, transforming themselves into the apostles of Christ. And no marvel; for Satan himself is transformed into an angel of light."

Notice the words "false apostles." This is a translation of the Greek word *pseudapostolos*, a compound of *pseudes* and *apostolos*. The word *pseudes* carries the idea of *any type of falsehood*. It can picture a person who either intentionally or unintentionally projects a false image of himself, someone who walks under some pretense, or one who projects an image that is untrue.

The second word — *apostolos* — is the term we've been studying since Lesson 1. It describes *one who is sent to others to take the Gospel to untouched regions and establish the Church.* Hence, the words "false apostles" in Second Corinthians 11:13 describe *a pretend apostle or someone who intentionally represents himself to be an apostle even though he knows he is not.*

False Apostles Are 'Deceitful Workers'

In verse 13, Paul also described these false apostles as "deceitful workers." In Greek, the word "deceitful" is a form of the word *dolios*, which was used to describe *bait that is put on a hook to catch fish*. It conveys the idea of *craftiness, cheating, cunning, dishonesty, fraud, guile*, and *trickery intended to entrap someone in an act of deception*. Like a fisherman who carefully camouflages a hook with bait, these counterfeit apostles lured sincere believers closer and closer until they finally took the bait. The moment unsuspecting believers swallowed their lie, the hook was set, and these false apostles began to reel in individuals and entire congregations until they were captive to their influence. Their deception was very intentional.

These pretend apostles are called *deceitful workers*, and the word "workers" here is a translation of the Greek word *ergates*, which depicts *someone who actively works at what he is doing*. The use of this word indicates there is nothing accidental about what false apostles are doing. Their deceptive actions are blatant and premeditated. These false apostles are putting forth great effort to impersonate genuine apostles with the aim of capturing people and pulling them away from someone else's apostolic authority and securing them under their own so-called authority.

According to Paul, these deceitful workers were so skilled at the art of deception they were able to transform themselves into what looked like real apostles of Christ. The word "transforming" in Second Corinthians 11:13 is the Greek word *metaschematidzo*, which means *to disguise oneself, to deliberately change one's outward appearance*, or *to masquerade in clothing that depicts a person as different than he really is*.

Here, Paul was referring to individuals who intentionally attempted to pass themselves off as apostles, knowing full well they were not. He alerted believers to this blatant act of deception to protect them — and us — from being misled and taken captive. He wasn't trying to create a spirit of suspicion but, rather, create a distinction between real apostles and false apostles.

The apostolic call is so important in building up the Church that those who imitate this call for the sake of personal gain should not be tolerated by any church leader or congregation. If a person has an authentic apostolic call, a test or a little scrutiny won't hurt or diminish his gift. In fact, it will simply establish and prove that he's genuine, which will open the door for you to receive him and to benefit from the rich blessings of his apostolic anointing.

In our next lesson, we will shift gears and begin our study of what a prophet is and how they operate in the Church.

STUDY QUESTIONS

> Study to shew thyself approved unto God, a workman that
> needeth not to be ashamed, rightly dividing the word of truth.
> — 2 Timothy 2:15

1. The words "false apostles" in Second Corinthians 11:13 describe *pretend apostles* who intentionally present themselves as apostles even though they know they are not. What is the primary factor motivating these individuals to make such a false claim?

    Jude, the half-brother of Jesus, had a great deal to say about these fakes and phonies slithering their way into the Church during the last days. Take a few moments to read what he wrote about them in verses 4-19. Identify their deceptive ways and take note of how God will deal with them. According to verses 3 and 20-23, what should be your response to these imposters?

2. In addition to the relational and territorial aspects of being an apostle, sometimes apostleship relates to a specific ethnic group. According to Acts 9:15 and 26:14-18, what did Jesus specifically call Paul to do? Of this call, what was his top priority? (Also consider Romans 11:13 and Galatians 2:7-9.)

3. In the early years of Paul's ministry, the Bible says he repeatedly did something every time he entered a city. What was that? (*See* Acts 13:4,5; 14:1,2; 17:1,2,10.) In Corinth, Paul began to do the same thing again, but then he made an abrupt change. What did he do, and what was the outcome of him aligning his priorities? (*See* Acts 18:4-11.)

PRACTICAL APPLICATION

> But be ye doers of the word, and not hearers only,
> deceiving your own selves.
> — James 1:22

1. What do you understand God's call to be on your life in your current season?
2. Be honest, are you doing what He's asked you to do? Are you keeping the "first things" first, or are your priorities out of line? What does Paul's example of repeatedly trying to minister to the Jews speak to you about the importance of keeping "first things" first in your life?
3. What type of fruit are your efforts producing? Are they marked with peace, joy, and success? Or are they filled with frustration, aggravation, chaos, and disappointment? What changes do you feel the Holy Spirit is asking you to make to come into alignment with His purpose for your life?

LESSON 10

TOPIC
What Is a Prophet?

SCRIPTURES

1. **Ephesians 4:11,12** — And he [Christ] gave some, apostles; and some, prophets; and some, evangelists; and some, pastors and teachers; for the perfecting of the saints, for the work of the ministry, for the edifying of the body of Christ.
2. **1 Samuel 9:9** — Beforetime in Israel, when a man went to enquire of God, thus he spake, Come, and let us go to the seer: for he that is now called a Prophet was beforetime called a Seer.
3. **2 Samuel 15:27** — The king [Saul] said also unto Zadok the priest, Art not thou a seer....
4. **2 Samuel 24:11** — For when David was up in the morning, the word of the Lord came unto the prophet Gad, David's seer....

SYNOPSIS

Just as there have been many people claiming to be apostles who are not, there are also individuals who've self-appointed themselves as prophets but are mistaken. Are there still genuine prophets operating in the Church today? Absolutely! Paul said that Jesus gave us the fivefold ministry gifts of apostles, prophets, evangelists, pastors, and teachers for the "…perfecting of the saints, for the work of the ministry, for the edifying of the body of Christ: Till we all come in the unity of the faith, and of the knowledge of the Son of God…" (Ephesians 4:12,13).

So what exactly is a prophet? What was the purpose of prophets in Old Testament times, and was their role any different in New Testament times?

The emphasis of this lesson:

Christ has emphatically placed all fivefold gifts — including the gift of the prophet — in the Church, and they are to be active until the end of the Church Age. The two categories that Old Testament prophets were placed in were hearers and seers. Seers have the divine ability of insight, foresight, and hindsight.

Jesus *Emphatically* and *Categorically* Gave the Fivefold Gifts to the Church

Let's begin this lesson by looking once more at Paul's words in Ephesians 4:11 and 12, which says, "And he [Christ] gave some, apostles; and some, prophets; and some, evangelists; and some, pastors and teachers; for the perfecting of the saints, for the work of the ministry, for the edifying of the body of Christ."

Notice the word "some," which appears four times in verse 11. It serves as *an exclamation mark* and would more accurately be rendered as *emphatically* or *categorically*. Thus, we could literally translate this, "And indeed, He gave some to be apostles, and indeed, some to be prophets, and indeed, some to be evangelists, and indeed, some to be pastors and teachers…." Or, we could translate it, "And He emphatically gave some to be apostles; and emphatically, some to be prophets; and categorically, some to be evangelists; and categorically, some to be pastors and teachers…."

So, Christ has indeed, categorically, and emphatically placed these five gifts in the Church, and they are to be active in the Church until the end of the Church Age. Regardless of what others teach or claim about these fivefold gifts, they are still meant for the building up of the Church today!

What a 'Cessationist' Believes

In the program, Rick shared how when he was growing up he was reared in a wonderful church that developed in him a very strong doctrinal foundation. They taught him to love Jesus, love the Bible, and love the lost, all of which he is very grateful for. Unfortunately, the denomination he belonged to were cessationists, which means they believed that the fivefold ministry gifts ceased to exist at the end of the Apostolic Age.

For example, they believed that the gift of the apostle ceased and there were no more apostles after the original Twelve passed into eternity. Likewise, they believed the office of the prophet and most of the gifts of the Spirit also ceased when the Apostolic Age ended. Basically, they believed all supernatural manifestations described in the New Testament ceased with the death of the 12 apostles of Jesus.

What is interesting, is that their beliefs about what has continued into the present were actually very selective. For instance, they held on to the belief that the roles of the evangelist and the pastor have continued, but the offices of apostles, prophets, and teachers have ended. Therefore, based on their beliefs, they only allowed two of the five gifts to operate in their church.

Not Everyone Is an 'Evangelist'

Looking back, Rick can now see that the gift of the prophet was manifesting in his church. They just didn't recognize it and chose to call those individuals *evangelists*. This practice was rather widespread among many denominations in the '80s and '90s — maybe you remember it. In those days, many believers thought that if you weren't a pastor, you had to fall into the category of an evangelist.

People like Kenneth Copeland, who really is a bona fide prophet, were categorized as an evangelist. He even called his ministry the Kenneth Copeland Evangelistic Association. But Kenneth Copeland was not an evangelist; he was a prophet. At times, even teachers weren't received as a teacher. It seems that any minister that wasn't a pastor was just lumped into the category of evangelists.

For years, when guest speakers ministered in different churches and held a "revival," they were called evangelists. But when they passionately preached to the church, calling people to turn back to God in repentance, they were not operating in the office of an evangelist. They were functioning as a New Testament *prophet*. They didn't preach to the lost and birth newborn Christians into the Kingdom. They preached to God's people and called them to repent and renew their passion for Christ. The alters were filled with church goers recommitting their lives to Jesus.

To be clear, an evangelist always manifests supernatural signs, wonders, and mighty deeds. That is not what prophets do. Prophets call God's people back into relationship with Christ and tell of future things to come. Unfortunately, because so many people didn't understand that the gift of the prophet has continued, those functioning in that gift were misclassified as evangelists.

Instead of being cessationists, we need to be continuationists. What is a continuationist? you might ask. It is one who doctrinally believes that all the fivefold ministry gifts and all the supernatural gifts of the Holy Spirit have continued from the Early Church of the First Century through today and that these gifts will continue till the end of the Church Age. It is God's desire and plan that these gifts will perpetually be active in the church. If you believe this to be true, you are a continuationist too.

What Is a Prophet?

Historically, the word "prophet" was a general term used by all religions — pagans, Jews, and Christians alike. It specifically was used to describe any person who served as *a conduit, a channel,* or *a voice for the spirit realm.*

When you read the Old Testament, you'll discover that there were several ungodly prophets, such as the prophets of Baal who served as conduits or channels for evil entities. For example, in First Kings 18 the Bible talks about 450 prophets of Baal who were pitted against the prophet Elijah in a winner-takes-all competition on top of Mount Carmel.

The point is that the word *prophet* was not a term used to exclusively describe one of God's prophets but a general term used in every ancient religion to depict any person who was a conduit, a channel, or a voice for the spirit realm.

In the Old Testament, there are two primary words used to describe a prophet to God's people, and each term signifies the specific way in which the prophet heard and received things from God. First is the Hebrew word "navi," which was used to describe *speaking prophets* who would largely receive or *hear* words and impressions from God that they were then expected to articulate to an audience of hearers.

Second is the Hebrew word "ra'ah," and it was used to describe *seeing prophets* or *seers*. This group of prophets saw things in the realm of the spirit or in their mind's eye. Both the *navi* and *ra'ah* prophets received prophetic insight from God, but this data was imparted in different ways. Nevertheless, the prophetic end result was the same.

Examples of 'Seers' in Scripture

A careful study of the Old Testament reveals that there were many godly seers throughout history. Again, these would be signified by the Hebrew word *ra'ah*. The Bible says, "Beforetime in Israel, when a man went to enquire of God, thus he spake, Come, and let us go to the seer: for he that is now called a Prophet was beforetime called a Seer" (1 Samuel 9:9).

The first seer noted in Scripture is the prophet *Samuel*. We find this in First Samuel 9:1-19 when Saul was looking for his lost animals and sought out Samuel for assistance.

When King David was running from his mutinous son Absalom, he spoke with *Zadok* the seer. Second Samuel 15:27 says, "The king said also unto Zadok the priest, Art not thou a seer...."

Later, when David rose and had all the able warriors in Israel numbered, another seer spoke to him on behalf of God — "For when David was up in the morning, the word of the Lord came unto the prophet *Gad*, David's seer..." (2 Samuel 24:11).

Who else is noted as a seer in Scripture? Here is a quick overview of a few:

- **Samuel** the seer (1 Chronicles 9:22; 26:28)
- **Heman** the king's seer (1 Chronicles 25:5)
- **Gad** the seer (1 Chronicles 29:29,30)
- **Iddo** the seer (2 Chronicles 9:29)
- **Hanani** the seer (2 Chronicles 19:2)
- **Asaph** the seer (2 Chronicles 29:30)

- **Multiple seers** who spoke to King Manasseh (2 Chronicles 33:18)
- **Amos** the seer (Amos 7:12)

All these seers were prophets (*ra'ah*) who had a divine gift to see things in the spirit realm. Often, through dreams and visions, they saw scenes or pictures of things no one else could see with the natural eye — things God wanted to reveal to them and through them.

Insight, Foresight, and Hindsight

Old Testament prophetic seers had the ability to understand the root issues behind situations and circumstances. They could accurately envision people's motives, agendas, and plans. Amazingly, they had the divine **insight** to see into a matter, evaluate the problem, and understand it in depth.

Once God made His insights known to a seer, that prophet was responsible to interpret it and declare it to his intended audience. Thus, in addition to having keen spiritual vision, prophetic seers had extraordinary understanding to counsel and provide wisdom and solutions to those whom they delivered God's messages.

Seers also had **foresight,** enabling them to see into the future and know what was going to happen beforehand. They had the visual acuity to predict events that would occur in the near or distant future. Furthermore, they also had prophetic **hindsight**, which was the ability to see and comprehend things that occurred in the past and know how they were affecting the present and could potentially alter the future. No one else could read the writing on the walls of a person's history like a prophetic seer.

Ancient Greeks Also Used the Word 'Prophet'

The Greek word for "prophet" is *prophetes*, and it was used with regularity by ancient writers in the secular Greek world. For example, historian and geographer Herodotus along with Plato, the renowned philosopher, used the word *prophetes* (prophet) to describe one with the ability to interpret the will of the gods.

Euripides, a tragedian performer and playwright, and Aristotle, a famous philosopher and student of Plato, both used the word *prophetes* to picture a divine expounder, a divine interpreter, or a mouthpiece for the gods and the spirit realm. Moreover, Sextus Empericus, who was a noted Greek philosopher and physician, used the word *prophetes* (prophet), to depict one who was a divine commentator.

The point is, the word *prophet* was not new to the Bible — Old or New Testament. Rather, it is an ancient word that has been employed for thousands of years by pagans, Jews, and Christians to describe people who are a mouthpiece for the spirit realm.

Moving forward, we will focus our attention on what the Jewish and Christian prophets had to say during their appointed times on the earth. Likewise, we will see that today there are still prophetic seers (*ra'ah*) and hearers (*navi*) who are active in the Body of Christ, communicating the word of the Lord to His people.

STUDY QUESTIONS

> Study to shew thyself approved unto God, a workman that
> needeth not to be ashamed, rightly dividing the word of truth.
> — 2 Timothy 2:15

1. Of all the prophets you know in Scripture, who is your favorite? What do you most admire and appreciate about them?
2. In the Old Testament, the two primary words used to describe a prophet are "navi" and "ra'ah." Briefly explain the difference between these words and tell the one thing — the most important thing — they have in common.
3. How vital is it for you to believe that the fivefold ministry gifts — and the gifts of the Spirit — are still in operation today? As you answer, consider Jesus' words in Matthew 8:13 and 9:29, as well as in Luke 8:48; 17:19; 18:42.

PRACTICAL APPLICATION

> But be ye doers of the word, and not hearers only,
> deceiving your own selves.
> — James 1:22

1. What did the church you grew up in teach regarding the role of the prophet? What does the church you're in now teach? Do they believe

in and embrace all the fivefold ministry gifts, or do they selectively believe that only certain gifts are still at work in the Church today?

2. The ancient word "prophet" is not new to the Bible but has been employed for thousands of years by pagans, Jews, and Christians to describe people who are a mouthpiece for the spirit realm. How does this knowledge change your understanding of this fivefold gift?

LESSON 11

TOPIC

Four Pictures of Prophets

SCRIPTURES

1. **Ezekiel 3:1-3** — Moreover he said unto me, Son of man, eat that thou findest; eat this roll [or "scroll" — i.e., God's message], and go speak unto the house of Israel. So I opened my mouth, and he caused me to eat that roll. And he said unto me, Son of man, cause thy belly to eat, and fill thy bowels with this roll that I give thee. Then did I eat it; and it was in my mouth as honey for sweetness.

GREEK WORDS

1. "prophet" — προφήτης (*prophetes*): a compound of the preposition πρό (*pro*) and φημί (*phemi*); the preposition πρό (*pro*) carries a wide range of meanings, and the word φημί (*phemi*) means to say, to speak, to communicate, or to shed light on a matter

SYNOPSIS

Situated in the Mount of Olives is an ancient tomb dating back over 2,500 years. In this remarkable and mystical place, several of the Old Testament prophets were laid to rest, including the prophets Zechariah, Malachi, and Haggai along with many of their prophetic disciples. Although their bodies are no longer present in the tomb, their graves and the surrounding corridors have been well preserved, and this area has become a sacred space for people to gather and seek the face of God.

Indeed, the prophetic ministry in both the Old and New Testament has been and continues to be a vital gift to the development and preservation of God's people. It is the second of the fivefold ministry gifts Christ gave to the Church (*see* Ephesians 4:11,12). So, what was the function of a prophet in the past, and is it still the same today?

The emphasis of this lesson:

The God-given role of a prophet is fourfold and is described in the meaning of the word itself. A prophet is one who lingers before God, receives God's message, and then stands in front of people to share that message — a message that sometimes includes the foretelling of future events.

The Meaning of the Word 'Prophet' Describes What a Prophet Does

As we saw in Lesson 10, the word "prophet" is the Greek word *prophetes*, and it is simply packed with meaning. It is a compound of the preposition *pro*, which carries a wide range of meanings, and the Greek word *phemi*, which means *to say, to speak, to communicate,* or *to shed light on a matter.* This lets us know up front that a prophet is a speaking gift — it is one who communicates on behalf of God.

The word *pro* — the first part of the word "prophet" — adds a wide range of meanings that are all critical in understanding a prophet's role. There are four ways the Greek word *pro* can be translated.

Number One: The Greek word *pro* means *before*. It pictures a prophet's position *before* the presence of God.

The primary role and responsibility of a prophet is to linger *before* the presence of God and listen with an open heart to whatever the Spirit of God would say to Him. The prophet lingers in God's presence to receive clarification, making sure he understands the exact message God is speaking.

As a prophet stays before the presence of the Lord, he humbles himself and sensitizes his heart to the Lord's will and voice, capturing the message God wants to communicate to His people. How does a prophet fully grasp what the Lord wants to speak? God's word to the prophet Ezekiel helps us understand what takes place. Ezekiel 3:1-3 says:

> Moreover he [God] said unto me, Son of man, eat that thou findest; eat this roll [or God's message], and go speak unto the house of Israel.
>
> So I opened my mouth, and he caused me to eat that roll.
>
> And he said unto me, Son of man, cause thy belly to eat, and fill thy bowels with this roll that I give thee. Then did I eat it; and it was in my mouth as honey for sweetness.

In this passage, we find that before a prophet can speak, he must first chew on and digest the message that God wants to give him. For a prophet to hear God's word and deliver it without first devouring and digesting every part of it himself is strictly forbidden. Before he can deliver the message in the power of the Holy Spirit, he must become intimately aware of every nuance of the meaning of what God wants to communicate. This shows the vital importance of a prophet staying *before* the presence of the Lord.

The word *phemi* — the second part of the word *prophetes* — indicates that eventually a time will come when a prophet moves from being before the Lord and listening to Him, to communicating the Lord's message to others — either a specific person or group of people.

Now, many people see a prophet speaking publicly and assume that he is prophesying spontaneously, but what they don't understand is the amount of time that prophet has spent lingering before the presence of the Lord. In fact, a prophet is only empowered to speak because he has spent much time *before* the face of God. He first speaks the message *before* God to make sure he knows God's heart and His word.

This practice of lingering before God in preparation for public ministry is true of every fivefold ministry gift. But the Greek word *pro* contained in the word *prophetes* (prophet) makes it abundantly clear that the chief occupation of a prophet is not speaking but *waiting before the presence of the Lord*.

Number Two: The Greek word *pro* means *in front of*. It describes a prophet's position *in front of* people.

A second translation of the word *pro* means *in front of*, and it depicts a prophet's public role to stand *in front of* people. The divine insights he receives from God are not for him; he is to impart them to those God asks him to stand *in front of*. He becomes the voice or mouthpiece of God to other people. When the word *pro* is compounded with the word *phemi* — which means *to speak* — it clearly indicates that a prophet is called to public ministry *in front of* people.

Once a prophet has heard and understands the message on God's heart — and has internalized and digested it for himself — he is dispatched from the solitary place before God to publicly stand *in front of* (the Greek word *pro*) people *to speak* (the Greek word *phemi*). His job is to give the message God has authorized him to deliver and nothing more.

To be clear, a prophet cannot move from listening to God to speaking in front of others until the Holy Spirit moves him to do so. Therefore, a prophet's first occupation is to be *before* the Lord in order to hear Him, to converse with Him, and to wait for the Spirit to move him to speak. And if God's message contains truths that are unpleasant to hear or difficult to consume, He still expects the prophet to deliver His message in the power of the Holy Spirit.

Once God has spoken to a prophet's heart and has given him a message, and once he has been released by the Holy Spirit to speak, then — finally — the prophet is able to move into the next part of his ministry, which is to stand *in front of* people and speak God's message. As a result, those who listen and are willing to fully receive what the Spirit has to say will be transformed. This is public prophetic ministry.

Number Three: The Greek word *pro* means *on behalf of*. Here, it describes a prophet's responsibility "to speak on behalf of" the Lord.

The word *pro* can also mean *on behalf of* and underscores that a prophet does not speak on his own behalf or on behalf of any other human being or organization. His job is *to speak* (*phemi*) *on behalf of* (*pro*) the Lord. A prophet does not have the right to speak his or anyone else's views or commentary or interpretation on a divine matter. He is to speak *on behalf of* the Lord and accurately represent God's words and God's heart. Thus, a prophet is to be a clear channel with a clear message.

As God's mouthpiece to the Church, a prophet must adhere to the message God has entrusted to him regardless of whether the listeners like it or not. Part of the prophet's ministry is to speak on behalf of God and address hot social topics and cultural concerns from the viewpoint of Scripture. It is vital for God's spokesman to speak up and communicate what God says on controversial issues in order to help God's people stay anchored in truth in spite of a world that is morally wobbling and, in many cases, free-falling into error.

Number Four: The Greek word *pro* means *in advance*. It carries with it the sense of a predictive ability and can be translated as one who "speaks in advance."

The word *pro* can also signify a prophet's ability *to speak* (the Greek word *phemi*) and predict or describe events *in advance* of their happenings. Although this is not what a prophet does all the time, it is a part of his ministry. The Spirit of God shows him *in advance* events that will take place in the future. This foretelling of things to come is clearly seen throughout the Scriptures.

Old Testament prophets foretold things, such as:

- **The rise and fall of kings and kingdoms**
- **The coming invasion of armies**
- **Seasons of economic blessing as well as economic hardship**
- **Periods of severe drought, great famine, and harsh weather patterns**
- **Times of captivity and times of freedom**

A careful study of the Old Testament reveals that God gave prophets the ability to see into the future and prophesy the coming of the Messiah. For example, the prophet Isaiah, who lived more than 700 years before Christ's birth, foretold with pinpoint accuracy the suffering Jesus would endure (*see* Isaiah 53).

The role of the prophet continued into the New Testament as well with individuals like Agabus, who prophesied a coming famine (*see* Acts 11:27,28). Likewise, both Paul and John prophesied future events such as the rapture of the Church, the coming of the Antichrist, and the events of the Great Tribulation. Thus, part of a prophet's ministry is *to speak in advance* of things that are coming.

A Quick Recap of the Role of a Prophet

Keep in mind, there are two kinds of prophets: those who are *hearers*, which is denoted by the Hebrew word *navi*, and those who are *seers*, which is signified by the Hebrew word *ra'ah*. Although the methods of receiving divine communication from God differ, the result of a prophet's work is the same. Here, again, is a quick summary of how prophets operate:

- First, the word *pro* means a prophet is to spend substantial time *before the presence of God*.

- Second, the word *pro* means after a prophet has been before God and has received God's message, he is dispatched to stand *in front of people*.

- Third, the word *pro* means that as a prophet stands in front of people, he speaks *on behalf of the Lord*, not on his own behalf.

- Fourth, the word *pro* means that a prophet sometimes speaks *in advance* of things to come.

In our next lesson, we will take an even closer look at how prophets do and do not operate.

STUDY QUESTIONS

> **Study to shew thyself approved unto God, a workman that needeth not to be ashamed, rightly dividing the word of truth.**
> **— 2 Timothy 2:15**

1. More than likely, you are aware of several prophets in the Old Testament. But what about the prophets mentioned in the New Testament? Read these verses and identify these prophetic voices in the Early Church. Notice how God used each of them as His mouthpiece.

- **Luke 2:25-35**
- **Luke 2:36-38**
- **Mark 1:2-8 and Luke 7:28**

2. One of the greatest prophetic messages in the New Testament is found in Matthew 24. As you take a few moments to reflect on this passage, identify the prophet speaking here and tell how God is using Him. Had you ever looked at this person as being a prophet before?

3. As we noted in this lesson, the New Testament speaks of prophets, such as Agabus, who spoke messages to the Church on behalf of God. According to Acts 11:27-30, what future event did Agabus predict,

and when did it take place? How did God use this prophetic word to move His people to action?

PRACTICAL APPLICATION

> But be ye doers of the word, and not hearers only, deceiving your own selves.
> —James 1:22

1. Of all the Old Testament prophets, name one that personally stands out to you and share how God used them to speak on His behalf. Did the people listen and receive God's message? What were the end results of this prophet's efforts?
2. As you finish this lesson, what are some of your greatest takeaways? What new insights about the ministry of a prophet did you learn?

LESSON 12

TOPIC

How Prophets Do Not and Do Operate

SCRIPTURES

1. **2 Peter 2:1,2** (*NKJV*) — But there were also false prophets among the people, even as there will be false teachers among you, who will secretly bring in destructive heresies, even denying the Lord who bought them, and bring on themselves swift destruction. And many will follow their destructive ways, because of whom the way of truth will be blasphemed.
2. **2 Peter 2:3** — And through covetousness shall they with feigned words make merchandise of you....
3. **2 Peter 1:20,21** — Knowing this first, that no prophecy of the scripture is of any private interpretation. For the prophecy came not in old time by the will of man: but holy men of God spake as they were moved by the Holy Ghost.

4. **Luke 2:25-27** — And, behold, there was a man in Jerusalem, whose name was Simeon; and the same man was just and devout, waiting for the consolation of Israel: and the Holy Ghost was upon him. And it was revealed unto him by the Holy Ghost, that he should not see death, before he had seen the Lord's Christ. And he came by the Spirit into the temple....
5. **Acts 11:28** — And there stood up one of them named Agabus, and signified by the spirit that there should be great dearth throughout all the world: which came to pass in the days of Claudius Caesar.
6. **Acts 21:8** — And the next day we that were of Paul's company departed, and came unto Caesarea: and we entered into the house of Philip the evangelist, which was one of the seven; and abode with him.
7. **Acts 21:10,11** — And as we tarried there many days, there came down from Judaea a certain prophet, named Agabus. And when he was come unto us, he took Paul's girdle, and bound his own hands and feet, and said, Thus saith the Holy Ghost....

GREEK WORDS

1. "feigned" — πλαστός (*plastos*): where we derive the word "plastic"
2. "merchandise" — ἐμπορεύομαι (*emporeuomai*): where we get the word "emporium," which is a place of commerce, a market, or a retail outlet; it also denoted a place where charlatans outwitted naïve buyers with sham products
3. "knowing" — γινώσκω (*ginosko*): to really know, to really grasp, or to really comprehend; it depicts a never-ending type of knowing or something that should be known, always known, and never forgotten
4. "first" — πρῶτον (*proton*): first, foremost, or above all else
5. "interpretation" — ἐπίλυσις (*epilusis*): a compound of the Greek words ἐπί (*epi*) and λύω (*luo*); the preposition ἐπί (*epi*) means upon and λύω (*luo*) means to loose, to set free, or to release; when compounded to form the word ἐπίλυσις (*epilusis*), it depicts a loosing or releasing that occurs at one's will; hence, the words "of any private interpretation" depict something that is loosed or released by one's own self — at will; thus, it pictures something that is self-loosed, self-produced, self-propelled, or self-generated by one's own will

6. "as they were moved" — φερόμενοι (*pheromenoi*): a technical word that was used in ancient times to denote a ship whose sails were set to catch the wind

SYNOPSIS

Because a prophet was such a powerful force in the Old and New Testament periods, at times frauds masqueraded as prophets in order to gain advantage over God's people. They knew that when they said, "Thus saith the Lord," it caused people to stand to attention. Consequently, these false prophets invented prophetic words to gain a following and to take advantage of the people's hunger and their respect for the voice of God.

This is exactly what the Holy Spirit prompted the apostle Peter to write about in his second letter. He reveals how prophets do and do not operate, giving us the vital information we need to recognize and reject the scam artists and embrace the prophets who are the real deal.

The emphasis of this lesson:

The primary task of a true prophet is to position himself before the presence of God. There in solitude, he learns how to hoist his spiritual sails and catch the wind of the Holy Spirit, speaking prophetically when God has something to say to His people.

A Vivid Picture of False Prophets

In Second Peter 2:1 (*NKJV*), Peter wrote, "But there were also false prophets among the people, even as there will be false teachers among you, who will secretly bring in destructive heresies, even denying the Lord who bought them, and bring on themselves swift destruction."

In this verse, Peter prophesies that just as there was a problem with false prophets in the Old Testament, there will be a problem with false revelators in New Testament times — including the last days — and they will secretly bring in destructive heresies. The words "secretly bring in" mean they will covertly and stealthily sneak right into the midst of the Church and bring unscriptural, profane teaching that produces destruction.

Peter went on to say, "And many will follow their destructive ways, because of whom the way of truth will be blasphemed" (2 Peter 2:2, *NKJV*). The word "many" here indicates that *masses of people* are going to be mesmerized and magnetically attracted to the ministry of false prophets. How will these fakes and phonies succeed in deceiving and leading many people astray? Verse 3 tells us, "And through covetousness shall they with feigned words make merchandise of you…" (2 Peter 2:3).

The word "feigned" here is the Greek word *plastos*, which is where we derive the word "plastic." Its use here gives us a picture of false prophets making up prophetic words on a whim, molding so-called prophecies to match whatever they think their listeners want to hear. Their motivation is not to bring a real word from God, but to make *merchandise* of God's people.

In Greek, the word "merchandise" is *emporeuomai*, which is where we get the word "emporium" from. It describes *a place of commerce, a market*, or *a retail outlet*. It was also used in the First Century to denote a place where charlatans outwitted naïve buyers with sham products.

Peter said at the very end of the Church Age, there are going to be false revelators who will manufacture phony prophetic words. At will, they will begin to mold their words like plastic into fake revelations to give their listeners whatever they think they want to hear. The reality is that this is happening right now. There are so many people online today bringing a prophetic word from the Lord, and many of them are false prophets. Be careful about who you're listening to. Before you "buy" what they're saying, you need to be assured these are authentic prophetic voices.

How Prophets Do NOT Operate

During the First Century, discerning false prophets from true prophets was quite a challenge. For this reason, the apostle Peter took time to address the issue in his writings. He said, "Knowing this first, that no prophecy of the scripture is of any private interpretation" (2 Peter 1:20). Here, he gives us a clear picture of how real prophets do NOT operate.

Notice the phrase "knowing this first." The word "knowing" is a form of the Greek *ginosko*, which means *to really know, to really grasp*, or *to really comprehend*. It depicts *a never-ending type of knowing* or *something that should be known, always known, and never forgotten*. The word "first" in Greek is *proton*, which means *first, foremost*, or *above all else*.

It is as if Peter is emphatically saying, "Know this, know this, know this! Never forget what I'm about to say to you. It is of utmost importance."

What did he want us to know and never ever forget? "…That no prophecy of the scripture is of any private interpretation" (2 Peter 1:20).

Now, there are a number of people who believe this verse means we should never interpret one verse all by itself. Instead, we should always compare a verse with other verses to arrive at correct scriptural conclusions. Although this is a true and advisable principle when studying Scripture, it is not Peter's primary focus. In this verse, Peter is not talking about biblical interpretation. He is telling his readers how prophetic ministry operates.

The fact is, when you look at this verse in the original Greek, it's quite different than how it reads in the *King James Version*. When Peter said, "…No prophecy of the scripture is of any private interpretation," the words "private interpretation" are a translation of the Greek word *epilusis*, which is a compound of the Greek words *epi* and *luo*. The preposition *epi* means *upon*, and *luo* means *to loose, to set free*, or *to release*. When compounded to form the word *epilusis*, it depicts *a loosing or releasing that occurs at one's will*. Hence, the words "of any private interpretation" depict something that is loosed or released by one's own self — at will. Thus, it pictures something that is self-loosed, self-produced, self-propelled, or self-generated.

Taking into account the original Greek meaning, here is the *Renner Interpretive Version* (*RIV*) of Second Peter 1:20:

> **You need to categorically know this and never forget what I'm about to tell you about true prophetic utterances. First, foremost, and above all else, you need to know and never forget that, emphatically, no prophecy of the Scripture is self-loosed, self-produced, self-propelled, or self-generated by one's own mere will.**

Grab hold of this truth because it is a profoundly important scripture regarding how real prophetic ministry does *not* operate. Essentially, Peter is saying genuine prophecy is *not* self-produced, *not* self-willed, and *not* self-projected. True prophets don't have the power to freely loose something at their own will. They are directed by the Spirit of God and Him alone.

How Real Prophets DO Operate

Immediately after Peter tells us how prophets do not operate, he tells us how they DO operate. He wrote, "For the prophecy came not in old time by the will of man: but holy men of God spake as they were moved by the Holy Ghost" (2 Peter 1:21). The first part of this verse affirms everything we just gathered from verse 20 — that genuine prophecy is *not* self-produced, *not* self-generated, nor does it come "by the will of man."

So how does prophecy come? Peter said "…holy men of God spake as they were moved by the Holy Ghost" (2 Peter 1:21). The key words in this verse are "as they were moved." This is a translation of the Greek word *pheromenoi*, which pictures something like a leaf being carried by a gust of wind or a small tree branch being carried by the current of a river. Neither the leaf nor the branch has the ability to move by themselves, which means they are totally dependent upon the wind or current in order to move. If the wind suddenly stops blowing, the leaf will fall to the ground. Likewise, if the current stops flowing, the branch will lay motionless in the water. Are you getting the picture?

Interestingly, this word *pheromenoi* — translated here "as they were moved" — is a technical word that was used in ancient times to denote a ship whose sails were set to catch the wind. If you think about it, the movement of ships was completely dependent upon the wind. But before a ship could catch the wind, the ship workers had to hoist their sails into position. By raising their sails, the workers made the ship ready to move the moment the wind finally began to blow. Although the ship workers couldn't produce the wind, they could prepare for it by having their sails ready to receive it when it showed up.

This is a beautiful illustration employed by Peter — a professional fisherman — to depict how true prophets operate. Just as sailors were totally dependent on the wind to carry their ship along in a forward movement, prophets are totally dependent upon the wind of the Holy Spirit. If there is no wind, there is no movement of the ship. Likewise, if the wind of the Spirit is not blowing, the prophet is silent. The sailors' job and the job of the prophet are the same: make sure the sails are hoisted and ready to catch the wind when it begins to blow.

Friend, true prophetic utterances are impossible without the movement of the Holy Spirit. If the Spirit is *not* moving, yet people are still attempting to prophesy, it is nothing more than the contrived utterances of men that are self-willed or self-projected. There is a vital lesson in this illustration for all of us. Whether we're a fivefold ministry prophet or an everyday believer, our job is to spend time raising our spiritual sails so we can move when the Holy Spirit says it's time to move. When the Spirit breathes and we're watching and waiting for Him to move, we will catch His wind and be propelled forward — not by our own self-will but by the will of the Spirit who has breathed on us.

A real prophet, therefore, is one who spends a lot of time and energy in the presence of God sensitizing his spirit to God's Spirit. That is, he has learned to continually hoist his spiritual sails, making sure that he's in position to catch the wind of the Spirit when the Spirit begins to move.

Just as there are times when a ship remains stationary, there will be seasons where there is no prophetic movement. When the wind of the Spirit ceases, the prophet cannot function. In those quiet moments, the prophet is to wait silently in the presence of God. In the stillness, there may be a temptation to fabricate something for the sake of excitement or to thrill a crowd, but this temptation must be resisted. Instead, he must listen for anything the Lord has to say and gather clarification on anything he believes he has heard. If a prophet has not spent time preparing his heart and mind to catch the wind of God's Spirit, he will not see much divine activity.

Two Examples of New Testament Prophets

The Prophet Simeon

The Bible provides a wonderful example of how a prophet operates in the life of a man named Simeon who lived in the city of Jerusalem at the time of Christ's birth. Luke captured an eye-opening snapshot of this man's life in his second chapter, saying, "And, behold, there was a man in Jerusalem, whose name was Simeon; and the same man was just and devout, waiting for the consolation of Israel: and the Holy Ghost was upon him" (Luke 2:25).

Early Church history tells us that Simeon was well known — even by the Jewish leaders — as someone who flowed in the prophetic. Luke confirms this by saying, "And it was revealed unto him by the Holy Ghost, that he should not see death, before he had seen the Lord's Christ. And he came by the Spirit into the temple…" (Luke 2:26,27). The fact that Simeon was led to the Temple by the Holy Spirit means he had his spiritual sails hoisted! When the wind of the Spirit blew, Simeon was moved by the Spirit to come into the Temple at the very moment Jesus was being dedicated by His parents. Thus, the Holy Spirit fulfilled His promise to Simeon and empowered Simeon to prophesy over Jesus.

The Prophet Agabus

Another example of how prophets function is seen in the life of a prophet named Agabus. The Bible says, "And there stood up one of them named Agabus, and signified by the Spirit that there should be great dearth throughout all the world: which came to pass in the days of Claudius Caesar." (Acts 11:28). Notice that the prophetic word — that a great dearth, or famine, was coming — was not self-generated by Agabus. It was given to him by the Holy Spirit.

Years later, the prophet Agabus showed up again — this time in connection with the apostle Paul. The Bible says, "And the next day we that were of Paul's company departed, and came unto Caesarea: and we entered into the house of Philip the evangelist, which was one of the seven; and abode with him" (Acts 21:8).

So, Paul and his traveling companions made it to the town of Caesarea and took up residence with Philip the evangelist, a man who had four daughters who flowed in the gift of the prophetic (*see* Acts 21:9). Luke went on to write, "And as we tarried there many days, there came down from Judaea a certain prophet, named Agabus. And when he was come unto us, he took Paul's girdle, and bound his own hands and feet, and said, Thus saith the Holy Ghost…" (Acts 21:10,11).

Isn't that interesting? The Scripture says nothing about Philip's four daughters speaking a word of prophecy to Paul. This lets us know the wind of the Spirit was not blowing on them at that time. Instead, the Spirit breathed on Agabus and moved him to leave Judea and speak a prophetic word to the apostle Paul. This demonstrates how real prophets don't self-loose, self-produce, or self-generate prophecy by their own mere will. Rather, they learn how to hoist their spiritual sails — staying still in the Lord's presence, sensitizing their spirit to His Spirit — so they are ready to move when He breathes.

The Renner Interpretive Version (*RIV*) of Second Peter 1:20 and 21

Looking once more at Second Peter 1:20 and 21, it says, "Knowing this first, that no prophecy of the scripture is of any private interpretation. For the prophecy came not in old time by the will of man: but holy men of God spake as they were moved by the Holy Ghost."

Taking into account the original Greek meaning in these verses, here is the *Renner Interpretive Version* (*RIV*) of Second Peter 1:20 and 21:

> **You need to categorically know this and never forget what I'm about to tell you about true prophetic utterances. First, foremost, and above all else, you need to know and never forget that, emphatically, no prophecy of the Scripture is self-loosed, self-produced, self-propelled, or self-generated by one's own mere will.**
>
> **But on the contrary and clear to the other side of the spectrum, authentic divine utterances were not carried or produced by man's mere willpower, wits, or initiative, but they were spoken by common people whom God touched, set aside, and consecrated for His own special purposes, those who learned to hoist their sails to catch the wind of the Holy Spirit. As the Holy Spirit moved upon them, they caught His wind and were enabled to speak and to move prophetically.**

Again, genuine prophets never move in their own ability or intellect. Just as ancient ships didn't move without the wind, a real prophet cannot speak prophetically unless the Spirit of God moves on him and empowers him to speak.

In our next lesson, we are going to look at what the Bible has to say about intertestamental prophets.

STUDY QUESTIONS

> Study to shew thyself approved unto God, a workman that needeth not to be ashamed, rightly dividing the word of truth.
> — 2 Timothy 2:15

1. What can a real prophet *not* do on his own? What is he totally reliant upon in order to move in the prophetic? Why is this so important?
2. Stop and think about the limitations of the prophet and what he needs to flow in his gifting. In what ways is your day-to-day life as a Christian similar? (As you answer, consider Zechariah 4:6; John 15:4,5; and Second Corinthians 3:5,6.)

PRACTICAL APPLICATION

> But be ye doers of the word, and not hearers only, deceiving your own selves.
> —James 1:22

1. Carefully read and reflect on Second Peter 1:20 and 21, along with Second Timothy 3:16 and 17. What connection(s) do you see between these passages, and what do they speak to you personally?
2. To help you identify and avoid listening to false prophets, read these invaluable words in Second Peter 2:1-3 and First Timothy 4:1,2 and 6:3-5. What are these fakes and phonies saying and doing? What has God vowed will eventually happen to them? What else is the Holy Spirit showing you in these verses?
3. There are many people online today bringing a prophetic word from the Lord, and many of them are false prophets. What prophetic voices are you listening to? Have you looked them up to see what they're about? Remember, be careful about who you're listening to. Before you "buy" what they're saying, make sure they are authentic prophetic voices who have a sincere heart to speak only what God is saying and not their own opinion.

LESSON 13

TOPIC
What and Who Are Intertestamental Prophets?

SCRIPTURES

1. **Ephesians 2:19-22** — Now therefore ye are no more strangers and foreigners, but fellowcitizens with the saints, and of the household of God; and are built upon the foundation of the apostles and prophets, Jesus Christ himself being the chief corner stone; in whom all the building fitly framed together groweth unto an holy temple in the Lord: in whom ye also are builded together for an habitation of God through the Spirit.
2. **Ephesians 4:11** — And he [Christ] gave some, apostles; and some, prophets; and some, evangelists; and some, pastors and teachers.
3. **Luke 2:25,26** — And, behold, there was a man in Jerusalem, whose name was Simeon; and the same man was just and devout, waiting for the consolation of Israel: and the Holy Ghost was upon him. And it was revealed unto him by the Holy Ghost, that he should not see death, before he had seen the Lord's Christ.
4. **Luke 2:36** — And there was one Anna, a prophetess, the daughter of Phanuel, of the tribe of Aser: she was of a great age, and had lived with an husband seven years from her virginity.
5. **Matthew 21:11** — And the multitude said, This is Jesus the prophet of Nazareth of Galilee.
6. **Matthew 21:46** — But when they sought to lay hands on him, they [the religious leaders] feared the multitude, because they took him for a prophet.
7. **Mark 6:4** — But Jesus said unto them, A prophet [referring to Himself] is not without honour, but in his own country, and among his own kin, and in his own house.
8. **Mark 6:15** — Others said, That it is Elias. And others said, That it is a prophet, or as one of the prophets.

9. **Mark 8:27,28** — ...Whom do men say that I am? And they answered, John the Baptist; but some say, Elias; and others, One of the prophets.
10. **Luke 4:24** — And he said, Verily I say unto you, No prophet is accepted in his own country.
11. **Luke 7:16** — And there came a fear on all [after seeing numerous miracles]: and they glorified God, saying, That a great prophet is risen up among us; and, That God hath visited his people.
12. **Luke 9:8** — And of some, that Elias had appeared; and of others, that one of the old prophets was risen again.
13. **Luke 9:19** — They answering said, John the Baptist; but some say, Elias; and others say, that one of the old prophets is risen again.
14. **Luke 24:19** — And he said unto them, What things? And they said unto him, Concerning Jesus of Nazareth, which was a prophet mighty in deed and word before God and all the people.
15. **John 4:19** — The woman [at the well] saith unto him, Sir, I perceive that thou art a prophet.
16. **John 6:14** — Then those men, when they had seen the miracle that Jesus did, said, This is of a truth that prophet that should come into the world.
17. **John 7:40** — Many of the people therefore, when they heard this saying, said, Of a truth this is the Prophet.
18. **John 9:17** — They say unto the blind man again, What sayest thou of him, that he hath opened thine eyes? He said, He is a prophet.
19. **Acts 3:22** — For Moses truly said unto the fathers, A prophet shall the Lord your God raise up unto you of your brethren....
20. **Acts 7:37** — This is that Moses, which said unto the children of Israel, A prophet shall the Lord your God raise up unto you of your brethren....
21. **Hebrews 13:8** — Jesus Christ is the same yesterday, and to day, and for ever.
22. **Acts 2:16-18** — But this is that which was spoken by the prophet Joel; And it shall come to pass in the last days, saith God, I will pour out of my Spirit upon all flesh: and your sons and your daughters shall prophesy, and your young men shall see visions, and your old men shall dream dreams: and on my servants and on my handmaidens I will pour out in those days of my Spirit; and they shall prophesy.

23. **Revelation 19:10** — …The testimony of Jesus is the spirit of prophecy.
24. **Ephesians 4:12,13** — For the perfecting of the saints, for the work of the ministry, for the edifying of the body of Christ: till we all come in the unity of the faith, and of the knowledge of the Son of God, unto a perfect man, unto the measure of the stature of the fulness of Christ.

SYNOPSIS

In the last three lessons, we have devoted our attention to the fivefold ministry gift of the prophet. We have seen that there were basically two categories of prophets — hearers and seers. We have also learned about the four aspects of the prophet's ministry, which are:

1. To spend substantial time *before the presence of God*.
2. To receive and understand God's message then be dispatched to stand *in front of people*.
3. To stand in front of others and speak *on behalf of the Lord*, not himself.
4. To speak *in advance* of things to come.

In our last lesson, we examined two passages from Peter's second epistle, discovering what a prophet does and does not do. Just as sailors were totally dependent on the wind to move them forward, prophets are totally dependent upon the wind of the Holy Spirit to move upon their lives. If the wind of the Spirit is not blowing, the prophet is to be silent. Thus, a prophet's job is to make sure his spiritual sails are hoisted and ready to catch the Spirit's wind when He begins to blow.

The emphasis of this lesson:

In addition to Old Testament and New Testament prophets, the Bible also speaks of intertestamental prophets. These individuals lived sometime after the end of the Old Testament and before the death, burial, and resurrection of Jesus and were instrumental in preparing people for His arrival.

The Fivefold Ministry Gifts Have Emphatically Been Given to the Church

Make no mistake: the Church is incredibly special to the Lord. So much so that the apostle Paul called it a habitation for the Spirit of God. He said,

"Now therefore ye are no more strangers and foreigners, but fellowcitizens with the saints, and of the household of God; and are built upon the foundation of the apostles and prophets, Jesus Christ himself being the chief corner stone; in whom all the building fitly framed together groweth unto an holy temple in the Lord: in whom ye also are builded together for an habitation of God through the Spirit" (Ephesians 2:19-22).

So, according to this passage, the Church — which every believer is a part of — is built on the foundation of the apostles and prophets, and Jesus Himself is the Chief Cornerstone. We are being molded, shaped, and fit together to form a dwelling place for the Holy Spirit to live.

Writing under the inspiration of the Holy Spirit, the apostle Paul went on to inform the Ephesian church — and believers of all generations — about the amazing ministry gifts Jesus gave to the Church. He said, "And he gave some, apostles; and some, prophets; and some, evangelists; and some, pastors and teachers" (Ephesians 4:11). We have noted in a previous lesson that the word "some," which appears four times in this verse is like an exclamation marker, punctuating an *emphatic, categorical* statement. Thus, this verse could be translated:

> "And He (Christ) gave *indeed*, apostles; and *indeed*, prophets; and *indeed*, evangelists; and *indeed*, pastors," and it's understood to mean "and *indeed*, teachers — no question about it."

You could also translate this verse:

> "And He (Christ) gave *categorically*, apostles; and *categorically*, prophets; and *categorically*, evangelists; and *categorically*, pastors," and it's understood to mean "and *categorically*, teachers."

Likewise, you could translate it:

> "And He (Christ) gave *emphatically*, apostles; and *emphatically*, prophets; and *emphatically*, evangelists; and *emphatically*, pastors," and it's understood to mean "and *emphatically*, teachers."

The apostle Paul's repeated use of this word "some" is the equivalent of him reaching through the pages of the Bible to grab hold of us and let us know that apostles, prophets, evangelists, pastors, and teachers are gifts that Christ has categorically, emphatically, and indeed given to the Church, and we should not question it.

The purpose of the fivefold ministry gifts is clear. They have been given to the Church "for the perfecting of the saints, for the work of the ministry, for the edifying of the body of Christ: till we all come in the unity of the faith, and of the knowledge of the Son of God, unto a perfect man, unto the measure of the stature of the fulness of Christ" (Ephesians 4:12,13).

The Intertestamental Prophets

The first prophets we find in the gospels of the New Testament are what we call *intertestamental prophets*. These individuals served in the role of a fivefold ministry prophet between the end of the Old Testament and the death, burial, and resurrection of Jesus. Although some people say that God was silent during the 400 years between the Old and New Testaments, He was not.

If you closely examine the so-called silent, intertestamental years, you will find that God never stopped speaking. Although He was not speaking through major prophets as He did in the Old Testament, He was, nonetheless, speaking. God has never been silent; He's always talking to anyone who has ears to hear what His Spirit is saying.

Unlike the prophetic voices of antiquity, the intertestamental prophets did not write scriptures. Still, they had a significant role to play in speaking about the end of the age and prophesying many of the things that we're witnessing and experiencing in our time. Here are three examples of intertestamental prophets talked about in the New Testament:

Simeon. In our previous lesson, we briefly mentioned Simeon, but did you know he was an intertestamental prophet? The reason he is placed in this category is because he lived between the end of the Old Testament and the death, burial, and resurrection of Jesus. His story is found in the second chapter of Luke's gospel.

The Bible says, "And, behold, there was a man in Jerusalem, whose name was Simeon; and the same man was just and devout, waiting for the consolation of Israel: and the Holy Ghost was upon him" (Luke 2:25). As Luke relayed his story, he opened with the word "behold" — the Greek word *idou*. This word describes *bewilderment*, *shock*, *amazement*, and *wonder*, and its use shows that Luke was simply shocked and amazed that this noteworthy man, Simeon, showed up the day of Jesus' dedication.

Some who are well-versed with ancient Jewish writers have noted that there was indeed a man by the name of Simeon who was alive and well known in Jerusalem at the time of Christ's birth. He was the son of Hillel, the founder of a major theological group. Simeon was so well known you might even say he was a celebrity-type theologian in Jerusalem.

Luke went on to say, "And it was revealed unto him by the Holy Ghost, that he should not see death, before he had seen the Lord's Christ" (Luke 2:26). The Jewish leaders at that time believed Simeon was endued with a spirit of prophecy and anointed to discern the signs of the times. According to the Scriptures, he was waiting for the consolation of Israel — that is, for the coming of the Messiah.

Anna. No sooner had Simeon finished blessing the holy family and prophesying Jesus' future that another intertestamental prophet came on the scene. Scripture says, "And there was one Anna, a prophetess, the daughter of Phanuel, of the tribe of Aser: she was of a great age, and had lived with an husband seven years from her virginity" (Luke 2:36). As we read the next few verses, we find that Anna was a devout woman of the Word who wouldn't leave the temple grounds lest she miss the moment when the Messiah would appear.

The Bible says she spoke about the divine revelation of the coming Messiah to all who embraced and gladly welcomed Him without hesitation or reservation. Every time the Holy Spirit led Anna to someone earnestly looking for and anticipating the Messiah, she opened her mouth and in the power of the Spirit, fanned into flames people's hopes and expectation of the coming King (*see* Luke 2:38).

John the Baptist. Another intertestamental prophet was the cousin and forerunner of Jesus, John the Baptist. John started his prophetic ministry at about the age of 30, and because of the radical nature of his work, many biblical writers compared him to the prophet Elijah. In fact, John's role was so prominent in Israel, he's even mentioned by the noted historian Josephus in his famous *Antiquities of the Jews*.

All four gospels include a description of John's groundbreaking efforts to prepare the way for Jesus to come. And the prophet Isaiah even foretold John's prophetic ministry, calling John "the voice of him that crieth in the wilderness" (Isaiah 40:3). Because John ministered after the end of the Old Testament era and before Christ's death, burial, and resurrection, John the Baptist was technically an intertestamental prophet.

The Greatest Intertestamental Prophet Was Jesus

Now, this may come as a surprise, but Jesus Himself is regarded as an intertestamental prophet. If you think about it, virtually all Jesus' prophetic ministry took place prior to His death, burial, and resurrection. The fact is, in addition to being an intertestamental prophet, Jesus operated in all five of the fivefold ministry gifts. We saw in Lesson 6 that He was known as the Chief Apostle, but Scripture also tells us unequivocally that Jesus was the perfect Evangelist, the perfect Pastor, and the perfect Teacher. Moreover, He was also, without a doubt, the perfect Prophet.

There are numerous New Testament verses identifying Jesus in His prophetic role. Take these passages, for example:

- **Matthew 21:11** — And the multitude said, This is Jesus the *prophet* of Nazareth of Galilee.

- **Matthew 21:46** — But when they sought to lay hands on him, they [the religious leaders] feared the multitude, because they took him for a *prophet*.

- **Mark 6:4** — But Jesus, said unto them, A *prophet* [referring to Himself] is not without honour, but in his own country, and among his own kin, and in his own house.

After Jesus sent out the Twelve, many began to question and speculate who He was. King Herod thought Jesus was John the Baptist who had risen from the grave. And according to Mark 6:15, "Others said, That it is Elias [Elijah]. And others said, That it is a *prophet*, or as one of the prophets."

At another point in Jesus' ministry, He turned to His disciples and asked, "…Whom do men say that I am? And they answered, John the Baptist; but some say, Elias [Elijah]; and others, One of the *prophets*" (Mark 8:27,28).

Like Mark, Luke also recorded Jesus referring to Himself as a prophet in Luke 4:24: "And he [Jesus] said, Verily I say unto you, No *prophet* is accepted in his own country." He said this while trying to minister in His own hometown of Nazareth.

After the crowds of people saw Jesus perform numerous miracles, Luke 7:16 says, "And there came a fear on all: and they glorified God, saying, That a great *prophet* is risen up among us; and, That God hath visited his people."

Luke also documented how people were divided over Jesus' identity, informing us that some were saying "…that Elias [Elijah] had appeared; and of others, that one of the old *prophets* was risen again" (Luke 9:8). Verse 19 is very similar, stating that the people "…answering said, John the Baptist; but some say, Elias [Elijah]; and others say, that one of the old *prophets* is risen again."

After Jesus was raised from the dead, He met two of His disciples on the road leading to the city of Emmaus. Noticing their dejected, hopeless state, Jesus began talking with them about why they were so depressed. When they asked Jesus if He knew about the things that had taken place, "…He said unto them, What things? And they said unto him, Concerning Jesus of Nazareth, which was a *prophet* mighty in deed and word before God and all the people" (Luke 24:19).

Again and again, people near and far called Jesus a *prophet*. The apostle John records the same kind of declarations in his gospel — pointing to the Samaritan woman at the well, a blind man that received his sight, and many others who had seen Jesus' miracles. Consider these verses:

- **John 4:19** — The woman [the woman at the well] saith unto him, Sir, I perceive that thou art a *prophet*.

- **John 6:14** — Then those men [Jesus' disciples who saw Him multiply the loaves and fishes], when they had seen the miracle that Jesus did, said, This is of a truth that *prophet* that should come into the world.

- **John 7:40** — Many of the people therefore, when they heard this saying, said, Of a truth this is the *Prophet*.

- **John 9:17** — They say unto the blind man again, What sayest thou of him, that he hath opened thine eyes? He said, He is a *prophet*.

Shortly after the Church was born, Peter preached to a crowd near the Temple and quoted Deuteronomy 18:15, saying, "For Moses truly said unto the fathers, A *prophet* shall the Lord your God raise up unto you of your brethren…" (Acts 3:22). Likewise, when Stephen stood up and spoke to the Jewish leaders, he declared, "This is that Moses, which said unto the children of Israel, A *prophet* shall the Lord your God raise up unto you of your brethren…" (Acts 7:37).

The Scriptures leave no room for doubt. Over and over, they proclaim that Jesus was the Prophet of God! In fact, He is still God's Prophet! Hebrews 13:8 declares, "Jesus Christ is the same yesterday, and to day, and for ever." Who He was in the past is exactly who He is today and will be in the future. He was a Prophet then, and He is still functioning as a Prophet in the Church now.

All Believers Have the Ability To Flow in the Prophetic

On the Day of Pentecost, when the Holy Spirit fell upon the 120 followers of Christ who were assembled in the upper room, Peter addressed the astonished onlookers and said, "But this is that which was spoken by the prophet Joel; And it shall come to pass in the last days, saith God, I will pour out of my Spirit upon all flesh: and your sons and your daughters shall *prophesy*, and your young men shall see visions, and your old men shall dream dreams: And on my servants and on my handmaidens I will pour out in those days of my Spirit; and they shall *prophesy*" (Acts 2:16-18).

Peter was quoting the prophet Joel (Joel 2:28,29), which tells us that both Joel and Peter affirmed that when the Holy Spirit was poured out, a new period of prophetic activity would be initiated in the earth, and that is exactly what took place.

In the Old Testament, prophetic dreams and visions were primarily given to the major and minor prophets, but when the outpouring of the Holy Spirit occurred, a paradigm shift took place. For the first time in human history, the Spirit of God began to take up residence and indwell every single believer! Therefore, in a sense, we are all members of a Churchwide prophethood.

We're told in Revelation 19:10, "…The testimony of Jesus is the spirit of prophecy." So any person who personally knows Jesus is enabled to some measure to function prophetically. The fact is, with the Holy Spirit living inside every believer, if God needs to speak a prophetic word to any individual or group, His Spirit can prophesy through any one of us — including you. Thus, we should expect and anticipate prophetic activity to continue and even increase until we come to the close of the age.

Of course, in addition to the gift of prophecy we as believers have through the Holy Spirit, there is also the fivefold ministry gift of the prophet, which is very distinct and separate from the common gift of prophecy. The fivefold gift of the prophet is what Paul mentions in Ephesians 4:11. The role of the prophet and the other fivefold gifts are meant "for the perfecting of the saints, for the work of the ministry, for the edifying of the body of Christ: till we all come in the unity of the faith, and of the knowledge of the Son of God, unto a perfect man, unto the measure of the stature of the fulness of Christ" (Ephesians 4:12,13).

In our next lesson, we will excavate the pages of the New Testament and uncover numerous examples of authentic, fivefold ministry prophets who served in the Early Church.

STUDY QUESTIONS

> **Study to shew thyself approved unto God, a workman that needeth not to be ashamed, rightly dividing the word of truth.**
> — 2 Timothy 2:15

1. How is Paul's description of us in Ephesians 2:19 and 22 similar to his words in First Corinthians 3:16,17 and 6:19 as well as Second Corinthians 6:16? Why do you think the Holy Spirit moved on Paul to repeat this theme? How do these passages instill a fresh, reverential fear of God in you regarding how you live?
2. Simeon and Anna are examples of what it looks like to eagerly anticipate the Lord's coming and to remain active while waiting. Take some time to reflect on their story in Luke 2:25-38. What can you learn from their lives and apply in your own life as you await Jesus' soon return to rapture us, His Church?

PRACTICAL APPLICATION

> **But be ye doers of the word, and not hearers only, deceiving your own selves.**
> — James 1:22

1. Prior to this lesson, did you see Jesus as a prophet? How about an intertestamental prophet? After reading through the numerous New Testament verses declaring Him to be a prophet, how has your perspective of Jesus been expanded?
2. In your own words, who would *you* say Jesus is? How has His presence in your life changed you?

3. The Bible says Anna spoke about the divine revelation of the arrival of the Messiah to all who embraced and gladly welcomed Him without hesitation or reservation (*see* Luke 2:38). Look around you. Who is the Holy Spirit leading you to that you can share the news of Christ's soon coming with? If you had only 30 seconds to share the Good News of Jesus, what might you say?

LESSON 14

TOPIC
How Many New Testament Prophets Are Actually Referred to in the New Testament?

SCRIPTURES

1. **Acts 13:1** — Now there were in the church that was at Antioch certain prophets and teachers; as Barnabas, and Simeon that was called Niger, and Lucius of Cyrene, and Manaen, which had been brought up with Herod the tetrarch, and Saul.
2. **2 Timothy 1:11** — Whereunto I am appointed a preacher, and an apostle, and a teacher of the Gentiles.
3. **Acts 11:27,28** — And in these days came prophets from Jerusalem unto Antioch. And there stood up one of them named Agabus, and signified by the Spirit that there should be a great dearth throughout all the world: which came to pass in the days of Claudius Caesar.
4. **Acts 21:8-11** — And the next day we that were of Paul's company departed, and came unto Caesarea: and we entered into the house of Philip the evangelist, which was one of the seven; and abode with him. And the same man had four daughters, virgins, which did prophesy. And as we tarried there many days, there came down from Judaea a certain prophet, named Agabus. And when he was come unto us, he took Paul's girdle, and bound his own hands and feet, and said, Thus saith the Holy Ghost, So shall the Jews at Jerusalem bind the man that owneth this girdle, and shall deliver him into the hands of the Gentiles.

5. **1 Corinthians 14:29-32** — Let the prophets speak two or three, and let the other judge. If any thing be revealed to another that sitteth by, let the first hold his peace. For ye may all prophesy one by one, that all may learn, and all may be comforted. And the spirits of the prophets are subject to the prophets.
6. **Acts 15:22,30,32** — Then pleased it the apostles and elders, with the whole church, to send chosen men of their own company to Antioch with Paul and Barnabas; namely, Judas surnamed Barsabas, and Silas, chief men among the brethren.... So when they were dismissed, they came to Antioch.... And Judas and Silas, being prophets also themselves, exhorted the brethren with many words, and confirmed them.
7. **1 Thessalonians 5:19** — Quench not the Spirit.
8. **1 Thessalonians 5:21** — Prove all things; hold fast that which is good.
9. **1 Timothy 1:18** — This charge I commit unto thee, son Timothy, according to the prophecies which went before on thee, that thou by them mightest war a good warfare.
10. **1 Timothy 4:14** — Neglect not the gift that is in thee, which was given thee by prophecy, with the laying on of the hands of the presbytery.

GREEK WORDS

1. "Now" — δὲ (*de*): an exclamation mark to make a powerful and dramatic statement; it means, "now amazingly..."
2. "signified" — σημαίνω (*semaino*): to signify, to give a sign, or to give an alert
3. "and" — δὲ (*de*): an exclamation mark to make a powerful and dramatic statement; now amazingly, emphatically, categorically...

SYNOPSIS

Can you imagine how the apostle Paul would react if he were alive today and saw how many people were calling themselves prophets? The growing list of individuals who promote themselves as a prophet on television, the Internet, and other forms of media is quite staggering. The truth is, only a handful of those who are called prophets today really are prophets. Most of them are using the term "prophet" incorrectly and are doing so simply because they don't understand what it means.

As we've previously noted, when a word is overused or used too loosely, its meaning becomes diluted, and that is precisely what has taken place with the word "prophet." Many goodhearted believers have a leaning toward prophetic things, but that doesn't make them a fivefold ministry prophet. Similarly, many have a leaning to help churches get started, but that doesn't make them apostles. The same can be said of the fivefold ministry gift of the evangelist, pastor, and teacher as well.

Nevertheless, you need to know that prophets are real and powerful, and there were many who functioned in the role of a prophet in the Early Church — more than you probably realize.

The emphasis of this lesson:

The New Testament lists several prophets — both men and women — who served in the Early Church. Some are named while others are not. These include local prophets as well as traveling prophets who journeyed in groups and often accompanied apostles as they were establishing the Church.

Barnabas, Simeon, Lucius, and Paul Were All Prophets

The book of Acts records many historical events of the Early Church, and in Acts 13, we see that God was doing something unprecedented in the church of Antioch. In verse 1, Luke wrote, "Now there were in the church that was at Antioch certain prophets and teachers; as Barnabas, and Simeon that was called Niger, and Lucius of Cyrene, and Manaen, which had been brought up with Herod the tetrarch, and Saul."

The first word — the word "now" — is the little Greek preposition *de*, which is an exclamation mark to make a powerful and dramatic statement. It is the equivalent of saying, "Now amazingly, there were in the church that was at Antioch certain prophets and teachers...." Indeed, the church of Antioch was a remarkable hub of prophetic activity.

Note that the names of five specific men are listed in Acts 13:1. Although the English translation doesn't specify exactly who were prophets and teachers, the Greek text uses certain parts of speech to indicate that the first three were prophets and the last two were teachers. This would mean Barnabas, Simeon who was called Niger, and Lucius of Cyrene functioned primarily as prophets, while Manaen and Saul functioned primarily as teachers in Antioch.

Then when we come to Second Timothy 1:11, we learn from Paul that his ministry calling expanded. He said, "Whereunto I am appointed a preacher, and an apostle, and a teacher of the Gentiles." The word "preacher" here is believed by some scholars to be synonymous with the word "prophet." Taking these two passages into account, we have four people standing in the office of a prophet: Barnabas, Simeon, Lucius, and Paul.

Agabus Was Also a Prophet

Another interesting passage regarding prophets is found in Acts 11:27 and 28, which says, "And in these days came prophets from Jerusalem unto Antioch. And there stood up one of them named Agabus, and signified by the Spirit that there should be great dearth throughout all the world: which came to pass in the days of Claudius Caesar."

Did you notice verse 27 says "prophets" — *plural* — came from Jerusalem to Antioch? And in this group of unnamed prophets was the prophet Agabus, who we mentioned in Lesson 12. The Bible says Agabus "…signified by the Spirit that there should be great dearth…" (Acts 11:28). The word "signified" is the Greek word *semaino*, which means *to signify, to give a sign*, or *to give an alert*. It pictures a dramatic foretelling of a coming famine that would impact the entire Roman Empire.

Agabus sounded this prophetic alarm "by the Spirit." The word "by" here is the Greek word *dia*, which means *through* or *through the instrumentality of*. This word indicates that Agabus was enlightened and empowered to speak *through the instrumentality of* the Holy Spirit. He had learned to hoist his spiritual sails so that when the Spirit moved, he was ready to move with Him. Thus, when the Holy Spirit revealed the coming worldwide famine, Agabus supernaturally caught wind of it and shared the prophecy with the Church. The believers in Antioch took the news seriously and collected a huge offering to be used by those in need. This prophetic word prepared God's people for what was coming.

Philip's Four Daughters Were Prophets

If you're keeping count, with the addition of Agabus, we now have five named New Testament prophets, plus the group of unknown prophets traveling with him. When we come to Acts 21, we find four more prophets mentioned, and all of them are women. The Scripture says, "And the next day we that were of Paul's company departed, and came unto Caesarea: and we entered into the house of Philip the evangelist, which was one of the seven; and abode with him" (Acts 21:8).

The Philip being talked about here was one of the very first deacons of the Church (*see* Acts 6:2-6). Over time, he had also become a fivefold ministry evangelist, and Acts 21:9 says, "And the same man had four daughters, virgins, which did prophesy." The opening word "and" is, again, the Greek word *de*, an exclamation mark to make a powerful and dramatic statement. Its use here means we could translate the verse, "Now *amazingly, emphatically, categorically*, this same man had four daughters, virgins, which did prophesy."

Clearly, these young women were well known for their prophetic, fivefold gifting. The fact that they are mentioned as prophetesses should challenge the false notion of some people who have said that the apostle Paul was against women being in ministry. There is nothing in this passage that would suggest that Paul or any of his companions had a problem acknowledging that these four young ladies were highly anointed of God.

So when Paul and his traveling companions arrived in the town of Caesarea, they took up residence with Philip the evangelist and his four daughters who flowed in the gift of the prophetic. Can you imagine the stories and supernatural insights they must have exchanged during their time together? Wow! It must have been an exciting visit.

The Holy Spirit Moved on Agabus To Speak a Prophetic Word to Paul

Our New Testament prophet count is now up to nine, plus the group of unnamed prophets that traveled with Agabus. Speaking of Agabus, Luke the writer of Acts, went on to tell us, "And as we tarried there many days, there came down from Judaea a certain prophet, named Agabus" (Acts 21:10). Again, Agabus reappeared, and like metal is attracted to a magnet, he was spiritually drawn to the house of Philip the evangelist and his four resident prophetesses. It was a common occurrence for prophets to be attracted to the company of other prophets.

It should be noted that there is no indication in the scriptures that Agabus knew the apostle Paul was staying at Philip's house or that Agabus was specifically going to Philip's house to give Paul a prophetic word. Yet, when Agabus arrived, the Spirit of God suddenly began to move on him. The Bible says, "And when he was come unto us, he took Paul's girdle, and bound his own hands and feet, and said, Thus saith the Holy Ghost, So shall the Jews at Jerusalem bind the man that owneth this girdle, and shall deliver him into the hands of the Gentiles" (Acts 21:11).

Isn't that interesting? Paul and his companions had spent several days with Philip and his four daughters that were prophetesses, but the Scripture says nothing about these women speaking a word of prophesy to Paul regarding the trouble awaiting him. This lets us know that the wind of the Spirit was not blowing on them. Instead, the Spirit breathed on Agabus and moved him to leave Judea and speak a prophetic word to the apostle Paul. This demonstrates how real prophets don't self-loose, self-produce, or self-generate prophecy by their own mere will. Rather, they learn how to hoist their spiritual sails — staying still in the Lord's presence and sensitizing their spirit to His Spirit — so that they are ready to move when He is moving.

No Prophet Knows and Sees Everything

So why would Philip's four girls be with Paul for many days and not see what Agabus saw? The answer is found in the apostle Paul's first letter to the church at Corinth, where he says:

> **Let the prophets speak two or three, and let the other judge. If anything be revealed to another that sitteth by, let the first hold his peace. For ye may all prophesy one by one, that all may learn, and all may be comforted. And the spirits of the prophets are subject to the prophets.**
> **— 1 Corinthians 14:29-32**

Notice in this passage the word "prophets" is plural, which means that in the city of Corinth, there was a group of prophets that were functioning in this gift. These verses also reveal that that no prophet knows and sees everything; no one has all divine revelation by himself. God speaks through many of His people, and we need the ministry of all of God's prophets in order to see the whole counsel of God.

Philip's four daughters were bona fide prophetesses who likely shared many prophetic insights with the apostle Paul during the many days he had been in their family's home. However, when Agabus arrived and gave the prophetic word from the Holy Spirit, they held their peace and made space for him — another prophet — to operate.

What Other Prophets Are Identified in Scripture?

Judas and Silas were prophets that accompanied Paul. Acts 15 documents that when a dispute broke out regarding whether or not new Gentile believers should be circumcised, the apostles and elders came together and then wrote to the Gentiles in Antioch what they believed the Holy Spirit was requiring. The Bible says, "Then pleased it the apostles and elders with the whole church, to send chosen men of their own company to Antioch with Paul and Barnabas; namely, Judas surnamed Barsabas and Silas, chief men among the brethren" (Acts 15:22).

We know from Acts 15:30-32 that Judas and Silas were there to deliver the letter to the believers in Antioch. Here, the Scripture says, "So when they were dismissed, they came to Antioch: and when they had gathered the multitude together, they delivered the epistle: Which when they had read, they rejoiced for the consolation. And Judas and Silas, being prophets also themselves, exhorted the brethren with many words, and confirmed them."

The church of Thessalonica also had prophets. We see in Scripture that there was another group of unnamed prophets functioning among the Thessalonian believers. In this case, these prophets were making a prophetic mess that the apostle Paul had to straighten out. That is why he wrote to the Thessalonian believers and said:

> **Quench not the Spirit. Despise not prophesyings. Prove all things; hold fast that which is good.**
> — **1 Thessalonians 5:19-21**

These instructions about how to deal with right and wrong prophetic ministry were not just for the believers in Thessalonica — they are also for us. *The Message* translation of this passage says it this way: "Don't suppress the Spirit, and don't stifle those who have a word from the Master. On the other hand, don't be gullible. Check out everything, and keep only what's good. Throw out anything tainted with evil" (1 Thessalonians 5:19-22).

There were prophets who prophesied over Timothy. When Timothy was discouraged, Paul reminded him of what was spoken over him at the time of his ordination. He said, "This charge I commit unto thee, son Timothy, according to the prophecies which went before on thee, that thou by them mightest war a good warfare" (1 Timothy 1:18).

Again, in First Timothy 4:14, Paul pointed to that same event, saying, "Neglect not the gift that is in thee, which was given thee by prophecy, with the laying on of the hands of the presbytery." Although we don't know the names of the prophets who were present when Timothy was ordained, we know that prophets were there functioning in their God-given gift.

Two end-time prophets will be operating during the tribulation. The Bible tells us that during the first half of the tribulation, there will be two high-profile prophets proclaiming truth from the city of Jerusalem. These two men will be so supernaturally energized by the power of God's Spirit that no one will be able to stand against them for three and a half years. At the close of their ministry, the Antichrist will be allowed to kill them, after which their bodies will be displayed in the streets for three days. On the third day, they'll be raised from the dead and ascend into Heaven with the whole world watching them as they depart.

Putting all this together, we have the specific names of 11 New Testament prophets in Scripture plus a whole company of other prophets that were active during this time that are unnamed. The point is, prophetic ministry is real, and it is a God-given gift to the Church. It has been in operation in both the Old and New Testaments and will continue all the way to the Second Coming of Christ. In our final lesson, we will focus on how to recognize false prophets and see why the Bible refers to them as "ravenous wolves."

STUDY QUESTIONS

Study to shew thyself approved unto God, a workman that needeth not to be ashamed, rightly dividing the word of truth.
— 2 Timothy 2:15

1. Did you know there was a prophet named Agabus mentioned twice in the Bible? Or that Philip the evangelist had four daughters that were

prophetesses? What is most intriguing to you about these individuals? (*See* Acts 11:27-30 and 21:8-14.)

2. Contrary to what some have taught and believe, women have been a vital and indispensable part of God's plan since Creation. What women in Scripture come to mind that God partnered with to fulfill His purposes and advance His Kingdom? Consider the examples found in Judges 4 and 5; First Samuel 1:1-28 and 2:1-11; and Luke 1:26-56 and 2:1-7, 21-24.

3. In this lesson, we examined 11 named prophets along with an untold number of unnamed prophets that are mentioned throughout the New Testament. What was most surprising to you from all that you learned? How has this enriched your understanding and given you a greater appreciation for the ministry of the prophet?

PRACTICAL APPLICATION

> But be ye doers of the word, and not hearers only, deceiving your own selves.
> —James 1:22

1. First Corinthians 14:29-32 reveals that no prophet knows and sees all. Why is this important? What would happen if one prophet did have all divine revelation in himself?

2. Have you ever been ministered to or given confirmation of direction through prophetic ministry? If so, briefly share what took place. What was the prophecy you received? How did God use it to encourage and direct your life?

LESSON 15

TOPIC

What About False Prophets?

SCRIPTURES

1. **Matthew 7:15** (*NKJV*) — Beware of false prophets, who come to you in sheep's clothing, but inwardly they are ravenous wolves.

2. **1 John 4:1** — Beloved, believe not every spirit, but try the spirits whether they are of God: because many false prophets are gone out into the world.
3. **Proverbs 24:6** — For by wise counsel thou shalt make thy war: and in multitude of counsellors there is safety.
4. **Ephesians 4:12,13** — For the perfecting of the saints, for the work of the ministry, for the edifying of the body of Christ: till we all come in the unity of the faith, and of the knowledge of the Son of God, unto a perfect man, unto the measure of the stature of the fulness of Christ.

GREEK WORDS

1. "wolves" — λύκος (*lukos*): a wolf or jackal; depicts wolfish individuals who come to attack, victimize, and take advantage of others
2. "try" — δοκιμάζω (*dokimadzo*): a test intended to prove the quality and trustworthiness of a product

SYNOPSIS

If something is real, you can know that the enemy will manufacture a counterfeit. Hence, just as there are real prophets, there are also *false* prophets. The same is true of apostles, evangelists, pastors, and teachers. Indeed, the Bible clearly warns us of...

- "False brothers" in Galatians 2:4 and Second Corinthians 11:26.
- "False apostles" in Second Corinthians 11:13.
- "False teachers" in Second Peter 2:1.
- "False prophets" in Matthew 7:15 and 24:11 as well as in Revelation 16:13 and 19:20.

In the Old Testament, New Testament, and today, there are those who are genuine prophets and those who are fake. But don't get hung up on the phonies. Yes, they're out there, but if you become so afraid of being duped by a false prophet, you'll become closed to the real ones and miss out on receiving what God has for you through them.

Think about it. Somewhere in society there is counterfeit money floating around. Fake twenty- and hundred-dollar bills are being produced and passed from place to place. But just because there are counterfeit bills in circulation doesn't mean you stop using money. That would be a foolish response. All of us need money to live, and therefore, we do our best to make sure we have authentic currency.

The same principle applies to prophetic ministry. God has given us, the Church, the gift of the prophet, and *we need it*. To reject all prophets just because there are false ones would be a grave mistake. Instead, we must learn how to recognize and reject the phonies and embrace and receive from the legitimate ones God has placed in our lives.

The emphasis of this lesson:

Jesus called false prophets ravenous wolves who spiritually prostitute themselves for some type of advantage or financial gain. God wants us to test the spirits operating through people who claim to be His mouthpiece.

False Prophets Are Like 'Ravenous Wolves'

Jesus — the Chief Prophet of all prophets — warns us, "Beware of false prophets, who come to you in sheep's clothing, but inwardly they are ravenous wolves" (Matthew 7:15, NKJV). The word "false" here carries the idea of *anything that is false, deceptive, or untruthful*. In this verse, it's compounded with the word *prophetes*, which is the word "prophet," and it pictures *someone who is bogus*. Interestingly, a "false prophet" in Scripture can describe a person who has been a false prophet from the beginning or someone who started out as a genuine prophet and became corrupt over time. This person has turned into a false representation of the Christ-given prophetic gift.

Jesus said that these false prophets are dressed in "sheep's clothing." This depicts a disguise that is intentional. In other words, false prophets are *knowingly* operating falsely, projecting themselves to be genuine and sincere while they are not. Jesus likens these kinds of people to "wolves," which is the Greek word *lukos*, describing *a wolf or jackal*. It depicts wolfish individuals who come to attack, victimize, and take advantage of others.

Now, we could stop right there and agree this kind of person is bad, but there's something else that's strongly implied in this word "wolves." During Jesus' day, the word *lukos* was a slang word used to depict *prostitutes* who wandered the streets at night, howling to get men's attention as they advertised their services and wares. Once they lured men into their dens of immorality and ensnared them, they seduced them and robbed them.

People living in New Testament times knew the word *lukos* ("wolves") referred to prostitutes. Thus, when Jesus said false prophets are like wolves, we could translate it, "False prophets are like ravenous prostitutes." Just as prostitutes prowled the streets at night to sell themselves and their sexual services for money, Jesus said false prophets prowl through the Church, looking for people to take advantage of.

Like prostitutes, these pretenders "prostitute" their services by giving so-called prophetic utterances for financial profit. By using this word "wolves" — the Greek word *lukos* — Jesus clearly taught that false prophets are those who spiritually prostitute themselves for some type of advantage or financial gain. Again, some of these individuals were false prophets from the beginning, while others started out genuine and pure but became corrupt after giving in to the lure of money and popularity.

What Are You To Do To Avoid Becoming the Prey of False Prophets?

God instructs us through the apostle John, saying, "Beloved, believe not every spirit, but try the spirits whether they are of God: because many false prophets are gone out into the world" (1 John 4:1). Because not everyone who calls themselves a prophet really is a prophet, we are to "try the spirits" to determine who is real.

We saw how the church of Ephesus "tried" those who said they were apostles, putting them through a rigorous test to determine whether they were genuine apostles or not (*see* Revelation 2:2), and Jesus commended the Ephesians for their efforts. In the same way, He wants us to "try the spirits" of those claiming to be His mouthpiece. The word "try" here is a form of the Greek word *dokimadzo*, and it depicts *a test intended to prove the quality and trustworthiness of a product.*

What's interesting is that this word *dokimadzo* was used to describe *an intense examination of individuals who were running for a public office to determine whether they had the right kind of character required to stand in a public position.* So a person couldn't just run for public office without first being put through a rigorous examination. Only after a person had passed a character test could they be allowed to compete for a public position.

Another use for this word *dokimadzo* — translated here as "try" — was to describe *the testing of coins to confirm they were real*. This practice came about particularly during the time of Emperor Nero. After the great fire of Rome, Nero needed a great deal of money to rebuild the center of the city, and he didn't have enough. To make up for the deficit, he minted counterfeit coins.

At first glance, these coins looked like real, silver currency, but only a tiny sliver was made of silver. The rest of it was fabricated from inferior materials. Because there were so many fake coins in circulation, a test was developed to determine whether coins were real or fake. Once a batch of coins was proven to be genuine, they were bagged and tagged to declare they had passed inspection and were genuine. All this meaning is found in the word *dokimadzo* — the Greek word for "try" we see in First John 4:1.

In the same way that people running for public office in the ancient world needed to have proven, impeccable character, those who stand before us in prophetic ministry need to be honorable and above reproach. Likewise, just as coins were tested to see if they were real or fake, we need to test the people in prophetic ministry to confirm that they are indeed genuine prophets. Essentially, that's what the Holy Spirit is telling us in First John 4:1, which says, "Beloved, believe not every spirit, but *try* the spirits whether they are of God…."

The Difference Between 'Wrong' Prophetic Ministry and 'False Prophets'

There's something else we need to understand, and that is there is a big difference between *wrong prophetic ministry* and being a *false prophet*. To help us grasp this truth, consider First Corinthians 13:12 where the apostle Paul wrote, "For now we see through a glass, darkly; but then face to face: now I know in part; but then shall I know even as also I am known."

This verse informs us that at this current moment, we all see through a glass darkly, and if we see through a glass darkly, that means no one sees everything perfectly clear. Thus, from time to time, even authentic, sincere prophets will make a mistake. As a matter of fact, there is not a single minister of the Gospel that gets it right 100 percent of the time. Every one of them have preached or taught something with confidence that he or she later regretted and possibly even retracted.

The fact is, as ministers grow and mature in the Lord, their knowledge and understanding increases, enabling them to realize what they taught earlier was incorrect. A minister who unknowingly presents something untrue is what we would call *wrong prophetic ministry*. Although their core motivation is to do their very best to hear from God and communicate His heart, sometimes they make mistakes.

The reason for wrong prophetic ministry varies. It could be that the person spoke out of his soul — allowing his own emotions, thinking, and desires to supersede the heart of God. A prophet may also speak in error because he is leaning on his own understanding. Or maybe he had a correct word from the Lord, but he didn't stop with what the Lord had said. Instead, he went on and added his own commentary. Whatever the case may be, just making a mistake does not equate a person with being a false prophet.

Staying in Relationship With God-Appointed People Protects Us From Error

The good news is that many of these unintentional errors are avoidable if a fivefold ministry prophet is in relationship with other fivefold prophets, teachers, evangelists, pastors, and apostles. Proverbs 24:6 confirms this, saying, "For by wise counsel thou shalt make thy war: and in multitude of counsellors there is safety." By being in relationship with other fivefold ministry gifts, a servant of God gives authority to other godly servants to speak into his or her life. This network of counselors forms a safety net to keep people out of error.

A danger exists when any fivefold minister becomes a "free floater" without any relationships with people who have authority to speak into his or her life. In the book of Revelation, Jesus compares His ministers to *stars* (see Revelation 1:16,20; 2:1). Stars shine light in darkness, and that is what His messengers — which includes all believers — are called to do.

What is also significant about stars is that they have a predetermined orbit, and they veer from it very little, even over thousands of years. In the same way that physical stars have a predetermined orbit, God wants His "stars" (or messengers) to stay in "orbit" — or relationship — with other fivefold ministry gifts.

What's interesting is that Jude calls free-floating ministers "wandering stars" (*see* Jude 13). These individuals may have started out as authentic, but somewhere along the way they strayed off track and were no longer accountable to the fivefold ministry people God appointed them to stay in orbit with, resulting in serious mistakes.

When spiritual leaders (or believers) stay in relationship with the people God has placed in their lives, four things happen:

1. They are submitted to authority and better enabled to stand humbly and soberly in a more authoritative role.
2. They are not free-floaters without accountability, but are established in a community of fellow ministers who can speak into their lives and ensure that what they are giving out has been tested and can stand up under the scrutiny of those with whom they are in spiritual relationship.
3. Their submission provides protection — both for them and those who follow them. It protects the prophet because he knows that if he does anything wrong, those with authority will bring it to his attention. Simply knowing that correction is possible is a strong incentive to stay on track and to weigh one's words before saying, "Thus saith the Lord."
4. Their submission to others also means the Church at-large can rest in peace, knowing that the prophet who is speaking to them is under the authority of seasoned voices who are speaking into his or her own life.

A Final Word

Friend, always remember the reason God has given us the fivefold ministry gifts of the apostle, prophet, evangelist, pastor, and teacher. They are "for the perfecting of the saints, for the work of the ministry, for the edifying of the body of Christ: till we all come in the unity of the faith, and of the knowledge of the Son of God, unto a perfect man, unto the measure of the stature of the fulness of Christ" (Ephesians 4:12,13).

The gift of the prophet and the apostle did not cease at the end of the Apostolic Age. They are still with us and at work and will continue till the end of the Church Age. By God's grace we can learn to discern who is real and who is not, and once we recognize those that are genuine prophets and apostles, we need to receive and embrace them, allowing their Christ-given gift to flow into our lives and into the Church.

STUDY QUESTIONS

> Study to shew thyself approved unto God, a workman that
> needeth not to be ashamed, rightly dividing the word of truth.
> — 2 Timothy 2:15

1. Because not everyone who calls themselves a prophet really is a prophet, we are to "try the spirits" to determine who is real. Carefully read First John 4:1-6 and identify the number one way you can recognize false prophets from real ones. Where do genuine prophets focus people's attention? With what does John equate false prophets?

2. Some prophets are fakes from the beginning, while others start out genuine and pure but become corrupt after giving into the lure of money and popularity. According to First Timothy 6:3-11:

   - **What motivates false prophets, and how does it contaminate their character and behavior?**

   - **What will happen to you if you focus on money and getting rich?**

   - **How should we view material possessions, food, and clothing? How about contentment?**

   Also consider Luke 12:15; Ecclesiastes 5:10; Hebrews 13:5,6; and Philippians 4:11-13.

3. Jesus compared false prophets to "ravenous wolves," which could be translated as *ravenous prostitutes*. Look at what the Bible says about prostitutes in Proverbs 5:1-14; 6:20-28; and 7:1-27. How might the wisdom presented in these passages be applied in your life to protect you from false prophets who prostitute themselves for financial and personal gain?

PRACTICAL APPLICATION

> But be ye doers of the word, and not hearers only,
> deceiving your own selves.
> — James 1:22

1. Staying in relationship with God-appointed people protects genuine prophets from drifting into error. The same is true of all believers — including you! What are some of the blessings of cultivating healthy relationships found in Proverbs 17:17; 27:17 and Ecclesiastes 4:9-12?

2. Who has God placed in your life that motivates you to grow closer to Him and fulfill His purpose for your life? When was the last time you expressed your appreciation and love to them? Why not take time today to call them or send a handwritten note to convey how grateful you are for them being in your life.
3. Be honest. Have you become so afraid of being duped by a false prophet that you've closed yourself off to all prophetic ministry? If so, you're missing out on receiving all that God has for you. Take a few moments to pray a prayer like this: *Lord, please forgive me for closing my ears and pushing away the gift of prophesy. I've been angered by those that are fakes and afraid of being tricked and misled. Help me to trust You and open my heart to genuine prophets You have placed in my life. I love You, Lord, and I thank You for helping me recognize and embrace the real and reject those who are false. In Jesus' name. Amen.*

Notes

CLAIM YOUR FREE RESOURCE!

As a way of introducing you further to the teaching ministry of Rick Renner, we would like to send you free of charge his teaching CD, "How To Receive a Miraculous Touch From God."

In His earthly ministry, Jesus commonly healed *all* who were sick of *all* their diseases. In this profound message, learn about the manifold dimensions of Christ's wisdom, goodness, power, and love toward all humanity who came to Him in faith with their needs.

☑ **YES, I want to receive Rick Renner's monthly teaching letter!**

Simply scan the QR code to claim this resource or go to: **renner.org/claim-your-free-offer**

WITH US!

🏠 renner.org

- facebook.com/rickrenner • facebook.com/rennerdenise
- youtube.com/rennerministries • youtube.com/deniserenner
- instagram.com/rickrrenner • instagram.com/rennerministries_ instagram.com/rennerdenise

www.ingramcontent.com/pod-product-compliance
Lightning Source LLC
Chambersburg PA
CBHW071714040426
42446CB00011B/2063